TOUCHSTONE

STUDENT'S BOOK 4A

MICHAEL MCCARTHY

JEANNE MCCARTEN

HELEN SANDIFORD

CAMBRIDGE
UNIVERSITY PRESS

CAMBRIDGE
UNIVERSITY PRESS

32 Avenue of the Americas, New York, NY 10013-2473, USA

Cambridge University Press is part of the University of Cambridge.

It furthers the University's mission by disseminating knowledge in the pursuit of education, learning and research at the highest international levels of excellence.

www.cambridge.org
Information on this title: www.cambridge.org/9781107624306

© Cambridge University Press 2005, 2014

First published 2005
Second Edition 2014

Printed in Hong Kong, China, by Golden Cup Printing Company Limited

A catalog record for this publication is available from the British Library.

ISBN 978-1-107-68043-2 Student's Book
ISBN 978-1-107-62430-6 Student's Book A
ISBN 978-1-107-63748-1 Student's Book B
ISBN 978-1-107-68275-7 Workbook
ISBN 978-1-107-62708-6 Workbook A
ISBN 978-1-107-69602-0 Workbook B
ISBN 978-1-107-66153-2 Full Contact
ISBN 978-1-107-67936-8 Full Contact A
ISBN 978-1-107-66763-1 Full Contact B
ISBN 978-1-107-68151-4 Teacher's Edition with Assessment Audio CD/CD-ROM
ISBN 978-1-107-61272-3 Class Audio CDs (4)

Additional resources for this publication at www.cambridge.org/touchstone2

Acknowledgments

Touchstone Second Edition has benefited from extensive development research. The authors and publishers would like to extend their thanks to the following reviewers and consultants for their valuable insights and suggestions:

Ana Lúcia da Costa Maia de Almeida and Mônica da Costa Monteiro de Souza from **IBEU**, Rio de Janeiro, Brazil; Andreza Cristiane Melo do Lago from **Magic English School,** Manaus, Brazil; Magaly Mendes Lemos from **ICBEU**, São José dos Campos, Brazil; Maria Lucia Zaorob, São Paulo, Brazil; Patricia McKay Aronis from **CEL LEP**, São Paulo, Brazil; Carlos Gontow, São Paulo, Brazil; Christiane Augusto Gomes da Silva from **Colégio Visconde de Porto Seguro,** São Paulo, Brazil; Silvana Fontana from **Lord's Idiomas**, São Paulo, Brazil; Alexander Fabiano Morishigue from **Speed Up Idiomas**, Jales, Brazil; Elisabeth Blom from **Casa Thomas Jefferson**, Brasília, Brazil; Michelle Dear from **International Academy of English**, Toronto, ON, Canada; Walter Duarte Marin, Laura Hurtado Portela, Jorge Quiroga, and Ricardo Suarez, from **Centro Colombo Americano**, Bogotá, Colombia; Jhon Jairo Castaneda Macias from **Praxis English Academy**, Bucaramanga, Colombia; Gloria Liliana Moreno Vizcaino from **Universidad Santo Tomas**, Bogotá, Colombia; Elizabeth Ortiz from **Copol English Institute (COPEI),** Guayaquil, Ecuador; Henry Foster from **Kyoto Tachibana University**, Kyoto, Japan; Steven Kirk from **Tokyo University**, Tokyo, Japan; J. Lake from **Fukuoka Woman's University**, Fukuoka, Japan; Etsuko Yoshida from **Mie University**, Mie, Japan; B. Bricklin Zeff from **Hokkai Gakuen University**, Hokkaido, Japan; Ziad Abu-Hamatteh from **Al-Balqa' Applied University**, Al-Salt, Jordan; Roxana Pérez Flores from **Universidad Autonoma de Coahuila Language Center**, Saltillo, Mexico; Kim Alejandro Soriano Jimenez from **Universidad Politecnica de Altamira**, Altamira, Mexico; Tere Calderon Rosas from **Universidad Autonoma Metropolitana Campus Iztapalapa**, Mexico City, Mexico; Lilia Bondareva, Polina Ermakova, and Elena Frumina, from **National Research Technical University MISiS**, Moscow, Russia; Dianne C. Ellis from **Kyung Hee University**, Gyeonggi-do, South Korea; Jason M. Ham and Victoria Jo from **Institute of Foreign Language Education, Catholic University of Korea**, Gyeonggi-do, South Korea; Shaun Manning from **Hankuk University of Foreign Studies**, Seoul, South Korea; Natalie Renton from **Busan National University of Education**, Busan, South Korea; Chris Soutter from **Busan University of Foreign Studies**, Busan, South Korea; Andrew Cook from **Dong A University**, Busan, South Korea; Raymond Wowk from **Daejin University**, Gyeonggi-do, South Korea; Ming-Hui Hsieh and Jessie Huang from **National Central University**, Zhongli, Taiwan; Kim Phillips from **Chinese Culture University**, Taipei, Taiwan; Alex Shih from **China University of Technology**, Taipei Ta-Liao Township, Taiwan; Porntip Bodeepongse from **Thaksin University**, Songkhla, Thailand; Nattaya Puakpong and Pannathon Sangarun from **Suranaree University of Technology**, Nakhon Ratchasima, Thailand; Barbara Richards, Gloria Stewner-Manzanares, and Caroline Thompson, from **Montgomery College**, Rockville, MD, USA; Kerry Vrabel from **Gateway Community College**, Phoenix, AZ, USA.

Touchstone Second Edition authors and publishers would also like to thank the following individuals and institutions who have provided excellent feedback and support on *Touchstone Blended:*

Gordon Lewis, Vice President, Laureate Languages and Chris Johnson, Director, Laureate English Programs, Latin America from **Laureate International Universities**; **Universidad de las Americas**, Santiago, Chile; **University of Victoria**, Paris, France; **Universidad Technólogica Centroamericana**, Honduras; **Institut Universitaire de Casablanca**, Morocco; **Universidad Peruana de Ciencias Aplicadas**, Lima, Peru; **CIBERTEC**, Peru; **National Research Technical University (MiSIS)**, Moscow, Russia; **Institut Obert de Catalunya (IOC)**, Barcelona, Spain; Sedat Çilingir, Burcu Tezcan Ünal, and Didem Mutçalıoğlu from **İstanbul Bilgi Üniversitesi**, Istanbul, Turkey.

Touchstone Second Edition authors and publishers would also like to thank the following contributors to *Touchstone Second Edition:*

Sue Aldcorn, Frances Amrani, Deborah Gordon, Lisa Hutchins, Nancy Jordan, Steven Kirk, Genevieve Kocienda, Geraldine Mark, Julianna Nielsen, Kathryn O'Dell, Ellen Shaw, Kristin Sherman, Luis Silva Susa, Mary Vaughn, Kerry S. Vrabel, and Eric Zuarino.

Authors' Acknowledgments

The authors would like to thank all the Cambridge University Press staff and freelancers who were involved in the creation of *Touchstone Second Edition.* In addition, they would like to acknowledge a huge debt of gratitude that they owe to two people: Mary Vaughn, for her role in creating *Touchstone First Edition* and for being a constant source of wisdom ever since, and Bryan Fletcher, who also had the vision that has led to the success of *Touchstone Blended Learning.*

Helen Sandiford would like to thank her family for their love and support, especially her husband Bryan.

The author team would also like to thank each other, for the joy of working together, sharing the same professional dedication, and for the mutual support and friendship.

Finally, the authors would like to thank our dear friend Alejandro Martinez, Global Training Manager, who sadly passed away in 2012. He is greatly missed by all who had the pleasure to work with him. Alex was a huge supporter of *Touchstone* and everyone is deeply grateful to him for his contribution to its success.

Touchstone Level 4A Contents and learning outcomes

Interaction	Skills				Self study
Conversation strategies	Listening	Reading	Writing	Free talk	Vocabulary notebook
• Use the present tense to highlight key moments in a story • Use *this* and *these* to highlight important people, things, and events in a story	**A lucky escape** • Listen for details in a story, and retell it with a partner **Facing a challenge** • Listen to a true story and answer questions	**Blind Chef Christine Ha Crowned "MasterChef"** • A news story about a woman who lost her vision and how she won a prize as a TV chef	**Facing a challenge** • Write a story about a time in your life when you faced a challenge • Format for writing an anecdote or a story	**An interview with . . .** • Pair work: Complete interesting questions to ask a classmate; then interview each other and note your partner's answers	**Mottoes** • Write down the verb forms that can follow new verbs, and use them in sentences
• Show understanding by summarizing things people say • Use *now* to introduce a follow-up question on a different aspect of a topic	**Broad tastes** • Listen for details and answer questions; then listen and choose the best responses **Keeping up with trends** • Listen to four people talk about trends, identify the topics they discuss, and answer questions	**How to develop your personal style** • An article about developing a personal style	**Style interview** • Write questions to interview a partner on his or her personal style; write answers to your partner's questions • Punctuation review: comma, dash, and exclamation mark	**What's popular?** • Group work: Discuss questions about current popular tastes and how tastes have changed	**Blue suede shoes** • Find and label pictures that illustrate new words
• Use expressions like *in fact* to sound more direct when you speak • Use *of course* to give information that is not surprising, or to show you understand or agree	**Away from home** • Listen to a woman talk about being away from home, and choose true statements **Favorite proverbs** • Listen to people talk about proverbs; number and match them with English equivalents	**Proverbs: The wisdom that binds us together** • An article about the study of proverbs	**Explain a proverb** • Write an article about your favorite proverb and how it relates to your life • Useful expressions for writing about proverbs or sayings	**Traditions** • Pair work: Ask *yes-no* questions to guess traditional cultural items	**Travel etiquette** • Find examples of new words and expressions you have learned in magazines, in newspapers, and on the Internet

Checkpoint Units 1–3   pages 31–32

Interaction	Skills				Self study
Conversation strategies	Listening	Reading	Writing	Free talk	Vocabulary notebook
• Check your understanding by using statement questions • Use *so* to start or close a topic, to check your understanding, to pause, or to let someone draw a conclusion	**Going out** • Listen to a couple discussing their evening plans **Extrovert or introvert?** • Take a quiz; then listen to a woman describe her social style, and answer the quiz as she would	**Examining the "Extrovert Ideal"** • A magazine article about a book on introverts living in an extroverted society	**Extrovert or introvert?** • Write an article about your own social style as an extrovert, an introvert, or a little of both • Uses of *as*	**Pass on the message** • Class activity: Play a game where you pass a message to a classmate through another classmate, and then tell the class about the message you received	**Get this!** • Expressions with *get* in context
• Organize your views with expressions like *First (of all)* • Use *That's a good point* to show someone has a valid argument	**We got robbed!** • Listen to a conversation; answer questions and check true sentences **Different points of view** • Listen to a debate, answer questions, and respond to different views	**Is your smartphone too smart for your own good?** • An article about online invasions of privacy	**Posting a comment on a web article** • Write a comment responding to the online article about privacy issues • Use *because*, *since*, and *as* to give reasons	**Do you agree?** • Pair work: Discuss controversial topics	**It's a crime!** • Write down new words in word charts that group related ideas together by topic
• Repeat your ideas in another way to make your meaning clear • Use *just* to make your meaning stronger or softer	**It's a small world!** • Listen to a story, and answer questions **Lucky or not?** • Listen to people talk about superstitions; decide if things are lucky or unlucky; write down the superstitions	**Separated at birth, then happily reunited** • An article about the true story of twins who found each other after growing up in different adoptive families	**Amazing family stories** • Write a true story from your own family history • Prepositional time clauses	**What do you believe in?** • Group work: Discuss unusual beliefs and strange events in your life	**Keep your fingers crossed.** • Use word webs to group new sayings or superstitions by topic

Checkpoint Units 4–6   pages 63–64

Useful language for . . .

Working in groups

We're ready now, aren't we?

Are we ready? Let's get started.

Haven't I interviewed you already?

I've already interviewed you, haven't I?

Where are we?

We're on number _____.

We haven't quite finished yet.

Neither have we.

We still need more time – just a few more minutes.

So do we.

One interesting thing we found out was that _____.

_____ told us that _____.

Checking with the teacher

Would it be all right if I missed our class tomorrow? I have to _____.

I'm sorry I missed the last class. What do I need to do to catch up?

When are we supposed to hand in our homework?

Excuse me. My homework needs to be checked.

I'm sorry. I haven't finished my homework. I was going to do it last night, but _____.

Will we be reviewing this before the next test?

"_____" means "_____," doesn't it? It's a regular verb, isn't it?

I'm not sure I understand what we're supposed to do. Could you explain the activity again, please?

Could I please be excused? I'll be right back.

Interesting lives

✓ Can Do! **In this unit, you learn how to . . .**

Lesson A
- Get to know your classmates using simple and continuous verbs

Lesson B
- Tell your life story using verbs followed by verb + *-ing* or *to* + verb

Lesson C
- Highlight key moments in a story with the present tense
- Use *this* and *these* to highlight information

Lesson D
- Read an article about a person who overcame an obstacle
- Write an anecdote about facing a challenge

Before you begin . . .

- In what way are these people's lives interesting?
- Do you know anyone who does things like these?
- Do you know any interesting people? Why are they interesting?

English Department News

Student of the month – MELIDA CORTEZ

How long have you been living here?
I've been living in Mexico City for five years. I came here to go to school originally. It's a great place to live.

Have you ever lived in another country?
No, I haven't. But my brother has. He's been living in Bogotá, Colombia, for almost a year now. I'm going to visit him later this year.

What kind of music are you listening to currently?
Well, of course I love Latin music. I'm listening to a lot of Latin jazz right now. I like to listen to music when I paint.

What's your favorite way of spending an evening? What do you do?
I like to go out with my friends – we go and eat someplace and then go dancing all night!

When did you last buy yourself a treat?
Last week, actually. I was at a friend's art studio, and I fell in love with one of her paintings. So I bought it.

What did you do for your last birthday?
I went home and had a big party with my family.

What's the nicest thing anyone has ever done for you?
Actually, about six months ago, I was complaining to my dad that I didn't know how to drive, so he paid for some driving lessons. I was thrilled.

Who or what is the greatest love of your life?
Oh, chocolate! I can't get through the day without some.

What were you doing at this time yesterday?
I was sitting on a bus. We were stuck in traffic for an hour!

You should really get to know **Melida Cortez**, a graduate student in our English Department. Also a talented artist, she spends her free time painting, and she started a sculpture class last month. She hopes one day to have an exhibition of her work.

1 Getting started

A Do you know someone that other people should get to know? Tell the class about him or her.

"You really should get to know my friend Frank. He's . . ."

B ◀))) 1.02 Listen and read. Do you have anything in common with Melida? Tell a partner.

Figure it out **C** Choose the best verb form to complete the questions. Use the interview above to help you. Then ask and answer the questions with a partner.

1. What book **do you read** / **are you reading** currently?
2. What **did you do** / **were you doing** for your last birthday?
3. Have you ever **been living** / **lived** in the United States?

2 Grammar Simple and continuous verbs (review) ◀)) 1.03

Extra practice p. 140

Simple verbs are for completed actions or permanent situations.		Continuous verbs are for ongoing actions or temporary situations.
Present	What kind of music **do** you **listen** to? I **love** Latin music. I **listen** to it a lot.	What kind of music **are** you **listening** to currently? I**'m listening** to a lot of Latin jazz right now.
Present Perfect	**Have** you ever **lived** in another country? No, I**'ve** never **lived** anywhere else.	How long **have** you **been living** here? I**'ve been living** here for five years.
Past	What **did** you **do** for your last birthday? I **went** home and **had** a big party.	What **were** you **doing** at this time yesterday? I **was sitting** on a bus.

✗ Common errors

Use the simple past for completed events, not the past continuous.

My birthday was great. My friends came to visit.
(NOT *My friends ~~were coming~~ to visit.*)

A Complete the conversations. Use the simple or continuous form of the verb in the present, present perfect, or past. Sometimes more than one answer is possible. Then practice.

1. A What _____*have*_____ you _*been doing*_ (do) for fun lately?

    B Well, I *'ve been taking* (take) kickboxing classes for the past few months. It's a lot of fun, and I *'ve gotten* (get) in pretty good shape.

2. A Who's the most interesting person you know?

    B Well, I _*think*_____ (think) my best friend is interesting. She ~~have been living~~ *lived* (live) in Europe for three years when she _*grew up*_ (grow up).

3. A _*Have*_____ you ever _*met*_____ (meet) anyone famous?

    B No, but last year, I _*saw*_ (see) a TV star on the street. We _*were*_ both _*waiting*_ (wait) in line for ice cream.

4. A When _*did*_____ you last _*exercise*_ (exercise)?

    B Actually, I ~~didn't~~ *have exercise* (not exercise) in months. I *'ve been* (be) really busy at work, so I haven't had time.

5. A What _*do*_____ you _*do*_____ (do) for a living?

    B Actually, I ~~don't~~ *i'm not working* (not work) right now. I *'ve been looking* (look) for a job for six months, but I *'ve not found* (not find) anything yet.

About you **B** Pair work Ask and answer the questions above. Give your own answers.

3 Speaking naturally Reductions in questions

*How long **have you** been learning English?* *What **do you** like to do in your English class?*	*Why **are you** learning English?* *What **did you** do in your last class?*

A ◀)) 1.04 Listen and repeat the questions. Notice the reductions of the auxiliary verbs (*have, do, are, did*) and *you*. Then ask and answer the questions with a partner.

About you **B** Pair work Interview your partner. Ask the questions in the interview on page 2. Pay attention to your pronunciation of the auxiliary verbs and *you*.

Building vocabulary and grammar

A 🔊 1.05 **Listen to Dan's story. Answer the questions.**

1. Where did Dan live before he moved to Seoul?
2. Why did he want to go to South Korea?
3. How did he get his job there?
4. What did his new company offer him?

LIVING ABROAD: Dan's story

Dan Anderson was born in the U.S.A. He's now living in South Korea. We asked him, "How did you **end up** living in Seoul?"

Dan: Well, it's a long story! Before I came here, I **spent** three years working for a small company in Tokyo while I **finished** doing my master's in business. To be honest, I wasn't **planning on** leaving or anything. But one day, I **happened** to be in the office, and one of the salespeople was looking at job ads online.

He knew I was **considering** going to South Korea someday – you see, my mother's South Korean, and I've always been interested in the culture and everything – and anyway, he leaned over and said, "Dan, this **seems** to be the perfect job for you. Check this out."

I looked at the ad, and I **remember** thinking, "Should I **bother** to apply?" But I **decided** to go for it, even though I didn't **expect** to get it, and to make a long story short, I got the job!

The company **offered** to transfer me to Seoul, and they **agreed** to pay for my Korean language lessons. I **started** working here two months later. And the rest is history.

I mean, I **miss** living in Japan, but you can't have it both ways, I guess. Actually, I can't **imagine** living anywhere else now!

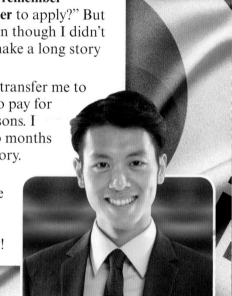

Word sort **B** Can you sort the verbs in bold above into the correct categories in the chart? Which verbs are followed by *to* + verb, verb + *-ing*, or a particle or preposition + verb + *-ing*?

Verb + *to* + verb	Verb + verb + *-ing*	Verb + particle / preposition + verb + *-ing*
happen (to be)	spend (three years working)	end up (living)
Seem (to be)	Finished (doing) / Miss (living)	Planing on (ing)
Bother (to apply?)	Be (planning) / Imagine (living)	
Decide (to go)	Be (considering) + ing	
Expect (to get)	Remember (thinking)	
Offer (to transfer)	Start (working)	
Agree (to pay)		

📓 **Vocabulary notebook** p. 10

Figure it out **C** Complete the sentences with the correct forms of the verbs given. Use Dan's story to help you.

1. I considered <u>studing</u> (study) electronics, but I ended up <u>doing</u> (do) math.
2. I expected <u>to graduate</u> (graduate) in three years. Then I decided <u>to change</u> (change) my major.

Grammar Verb complements: verb + *-ing* or *to* + verb 🔊 1.06

Extra practice p. 140

Verb + verb + *-ing*: consider finish imagine miss mind spend (time)	I **finished doing** my master's in business. I **spent** three years **working** in Tokyo.
Verb + particle / preposition + verb + *-ing*: end up keep on think about plan on	How did you **end up living** here? I wasn't **planning on leaving** Japan.
Verb + *to* + verb: agree decide happen offer seem intend expect	They **agreed to pay** for Korean lessons. I didn't **expect to get** the job.
Verb + *-ing* or *to* + verb with the same meaning: begin bother continue start like love hate	Should I **bother applying**? Should I **bother to apply**?
Verb + *-ing* or *to* + verb with a different meaning: remember stop try	I **stopped talking** to him. (We don't talk now.) I **stopped to talk** to him. (I stopped walking.)

A Complete the conversations with the correct forms of the verbs given. Then practice with a partner.

> **In conversation**
>
> *Begin, bother, continue, like, love,* and *hate* are followed more often by *to* + verb. *Start* is followed more often by verb + *-ing*.

1. A How did you end up _studying_ (study) here?

   B My friend recommended this school. I remember
   thinking (think) his English was good, so I decided
   to sign up (sign up) for this class. How about you?

   A Well, I wasn't planning on _learning_ (learn) English,
   but my company offered _to pay_ (pay) for my classes.
   I agreed _to come_ (come), and here I am! I want to
   keep on _taking_ (take) classes if I can.

> **Common errors**
>
> Don't use *to* + verb after these verbs.
> *I finished read**ing** the ad.* (NOT . . . *to read*)
> *I considered apply**ing**.* (NOT . . . *to apply*)
> *I don't mind work**ing** hard.* (NOT . . . *to work*)

2. A What are you thinking about _doing_ (do) next summer?

   B Well, it depends. I just started _working_ (work) in a new job, so I don't expect _to get_ (get)
   much vacation time. I intend _to take_ (take) a couple of long weekends off, though. You have
   to stop _to work_ (work) occasionally! Anyway, I love _surfing_ (surf), so I hope I can spend a
   weekend _visiting_ (visit) my cousins at the beach, too.

About you **B** **Pair work** Take turns asking the questions. Give your own answers.

Talk about it Why did you stop doing that?

Pair work Take turns asking each other questions using the ideas below. Ask follow-up questions.

Can you think of someone you . . . ?

▸ don't miss seeing
▸ expect to see next week
▸ happened to run into recently →encontrarte derepnte
▸ intended to see but didn't
▸ keep on calling
▸ love to hang out with

"I don't miss seeing my old math teacher."

Can you think of something that you . . . ?

▸ agreed to do recently
▸ are considering doing soon
▸ can't imagine doing in the future
▸ finished doing recently
▸ never bother to do
▸ stopped doing recently

"Why's that? Were you bad at math?"

🔊 **Sounds right** p. 137

1 Conversation strategy Highlighting key moments in a story

A Think of a time when you got lost. What happened? Tell the class.

B ◀))) 1.07 Listen. How did Mateo and Bryan get lost?

Mateo	Remember that time we were hiking in Utah?
Bryan	When we got lost? That was funny.
Kim	Why? What happened?
Mateo	We were on this trail, and it was getting dark. Then Bryan says, "Where are we?"
Bryan	Yeah, we couldn't see a thing, and we walked off the trail. It was that bad.
Mateo	Yeah, there were all these trees around us, and we were so lost. And we're thinking, "Oh, no." And we're both getting kind of scared. We just wanted to get out of there.
Kim	I bet.
Mateo	And Bryan says, "Should we jog a little?" And I go, "Yeah. I was thinking the same thing. Let's go."
Bryan	So we started jogging, . . .
Mateo	And we said to each other, "We've got to stick together, in case anything happens."

C Notice how Mateo changes to the present tense at key moments in his story. It makes them more "dramatic." Find more examples in the conversation.

"We're both getting kind of scared."

D ◀))) 1.08 Read more of their conversation. Change the underlined verbs to the simple present or present continuous to make the story more dramatic. Then listen and check your answers.

Bryan   Yeah. And all of a sudden, we ~~heard~~ *hear* this noise.
Mateo   And I ~~looked~~ over at Bryan, and I ~~saw~~ his face ~~was~~ white, and he ~~was starting~~ to run fast.
Bryan   Well, yeah. I mean, it was a weird noise.
Mateo   So, I ~~was~~ thinking, "Wait a minute. What happened to our plan to stick together?" So I ~~started~~ to run with him.
Bryan   Yeah, we ~~were running~~ through the trees, scared to death. It was hilarious! It was just like in a movie.

2 Strategy plus *this* and *these* in stories

[handwritten: sing] over *this*, *[handwritten: plural]* over *these*

When you tell stories, you can use *this* and *these* to highlight important people, things, and events.

> We were on this trail, . . .

> There were all these trees . . .

A Replace *a*, *an*, and *some* with *this* or *these* in the story below. Then take turns telling the story with a partner.

> "I have **a** *[handwritten: one]* friend who's always getting into funny situations. One time she was invited to **a** *[handwritten: her first]* going-away party, and she ended up getting totally lost and wandering around a neighborhood she didn't know. Anyway, she finally sees **a** *[handwritten: this]* house with **some** *[handwritten: these]* cars outside, and **some** *[handwritten: these]* people were barbecuing in the backyard. So she knocks on the door, and **a** *[handwritten: this]* nice guy lets her in. He thought she was one of his wife's friends. Anyway, she spent about an hour talking to **some** people before **some** guys bring out a big birthday cake and candles and everything. Then she finally realized it was the wrong party!"

About you **B** **Pair work** Tell about a time you or a friend got into a funny situation.

3 Listening and strategies A lucky escape

A You're going to hear a story about a skiing accident. Aaron was skiing with friends when one of them fell down the mountain. Circle four questions you want to ask Aaron.

1. Where were you skiing? *[handwritten: Alpes Iho 12000 12100 feet]*
2. How far did your friend fall? *[handwritten: 300 feet]*
3. What did you do when he fell? *[handwritten: get him]*
4. How badly was he hurt? *[handwritten: not much]*

5. Did you get help? How? *[handwritten: Rescue team]*
6. Did he have to go to the hospital? *[handwritten: Yes, in helicopter]*
7. When did this happen? *[handwritten: 3 4 months ago]*
8. Is he OK now? *[handwritten: Yes, he recovered few bounds head]*

B 🔊 1.09 Listen. Write answers to the questions you chose. Then share answers with a partner. Can you remember the entire story together?

About you **C** **Pair work** Think of a time when something went wrong or when you or someone you know had an accident. Tell a partner the story.

> "*. . . And suddenly she falls off the climbing wall and lands next to this guy. And all these people run over to see if she's hurt. She was OK. A little embarrassed, but OK!*"

Reading

A What kinds of competitions are there on TV shows? Do you ever watch them?

B Read the article. What was Christine Ha's disadvantage in the MasterChef competition? What advantage did she have?

> **Reading tip**
> Read the quotes in a news story first. They often give you a quick summary of the article.

Blind Chef Christine Ha
Crowned "MasterChef"

From the moment she took those first tentative steps onto the national stage, amateur chef Christine Ha captured America's heart.

During the season 3 "MasterChef" finale, Ha won the title, $250,000, and a cookbook deal, beating out about 100 other home chefs. But that's not what makes her so inspiring. Ha is blind – the first blind contestant on the show.

"I think there are a lot of people who completely discounted me," Ha said. "People will say, 'What is she doing? Is she going to cut her finger off?' But I cooked at home for years without vision, so if I can do it at home, I don't see why I can't prove to everyone else I can do it on national TV."

Week after week, the 33-year-old, who lives in Houston, Texas, managed to whip up culinary masterpieces with only her senses of taste, smell, and touch to guide her.

"I couldn't see what anyone else was doing, I was solely focused on myself, and I think that helped me. It gave me an advantage," she said. "When I came out of it, it was the most stressful, intense experience of my life, it was amazing."

Ha lost nearly all of her eyesight about five years ago after being diagnosed with an autoimmune disease that attacks the optic nerves.

"When I lost my vision, there was one time I tried to make a peanut butter and jelly sandwich," she said. "I recall getting it all over the counter. I just started crying and was wondering if I would ever cook again."

But she did more than pick herself up off the counter. She started her own blog, which is how the producers of "MasterChef" discovered her.

Now an official "MasterChef," Ha said, "I just want people to realize that they have it in themselves if they really want to. If they have that passion, that fire, that drive, that desire . . . you can overcome any obstacle and any challenges to really achieve what you want and prove yourself to the world. Everyone is very capable. Much more capable than they think they are."

C Find the words below in the article. Which of the two meanings is used in the article? Circle *a* or *b*. Then compare with a partner.

1. tentative
   a. not final
   b.) not certain or confident

2. a cookbook deal
   a. the chance to publish her own cookbook
   b. free cookbooks

3. beating out
   a. mixing rapidly in a bowl
   b. winning against

4. discounted
   a. reduced the price
   b. did not consider seriously

5. whip up
   a. make quickly and easily
   b. mix quickly until light and fluffy

6. pick herself up
   a. stand up after falling down
   b. recover from a difficult situation

7. drive
   a. determination
   b. use a car

8. overcome any obstacle
   a. beat or solve a problem
   b. climb over something that's in the way

D Read the article again and answer these questions. Compare your answers with a partner.

1. Why do you think Ha "captured America's heart"? Has she captured yours from your reading of the article?

2. After losing her vision, what did Ha try to do in the kitchen? In what way is this anecdote significant?

3. What do you think Ha means by "people have it in themselves"? Do you agree with her view?

2 Listening and writing Facing a challenge

A 🔊 1.10 Listen to a podcast about Bethany Hamilton. Complete the sentences with the correct information. Choose *a*, *b*, or *c*.

1. As a child, Bethany surfed almost every day with __*b*__ .
   a. her parents   b. her friend Alana   c. Alana's father

2. Bethany decided to return to surfing _____ after the shark attack.
   a. a couple of weeks   b. a month   c. three months

3. Bethany managed to stay on her surfboard because _____ added a handle.
   a. her mother   b. her father   c. Alana's father

4. In the World Junior Championship, Bethany took _____ place.
   a. first   b. second   c. fifth

5. Since Bethany lost her arm, she has _____ .
   a. written a book   b. starred in a movie   c. received help from a charity

6. Bethany is described above all else as a great _____ .
   a. athlete   b. role model   c. traveler

About you **B** Pair work Think about a time in your life when you faced a challenge. How did you feel? Did someone help you? How did you feel afterward?

C Read the story and the Help note. Then write a story about your challenge.

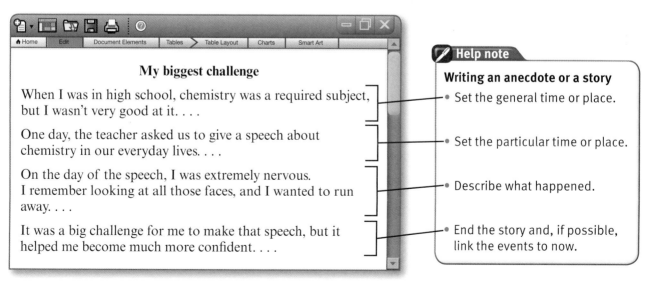

My biggest challenge

When I was in high school, chemistry was a required subject, but I wasn't very good at it. . . .

One day, the teacher asked us to give a speech about chemistry in our everyday lives. . . .

On the day of the speech, I was extremely nervous. I remember looking at all those faces, and I wanted to run away. . . .

It was a big challenge for me to make that speech, but it helped me become much more confident. . . .

Help note

Writing an anecdote or a story

• Set the general time or place.

• Set the particular time or place.

• Describe what happened.

• End the story and, if possible, link the events to now.

D Pair work Read a partner's story. Then ask questions to find out more about the story.

Free talk, p. 129

Learning tip *Verb patterns*

When you learn a new verb, write down the verb form(s) that can follow it. Then use it in a sentence. For example:

imagine verb + -ing	*I can't imagine having lots of money.*
decide to + verb	*I've decided to be a doctor.*
start verb + -ing	*I'm going to start saving money.*
start to + verb	*I'm going to start to save money.*

1 Write down the form(s) of the verbs that can follow the verbs below. Then complete the mottoes. Use the correct form(s) of the verbs given.

1. agree ___to + verb___ "Never agree _to lend_ (lend) money to strangers."
2. intend ___to + v___ "If you don't intend _to do_ (do) something properly,
    bother ___ing / to+v___ don't bother _starting_ (start) it!" _correctly_
3. stop ___ing___ "Never stop _doing_ (do) the things you
    enjoy ___to + ing___ enjoy _doing_ (do)."
4. keep on ___ing___ "Keep on _trying_ (try) until you find success."
5. consider ___ing___ "Consider _taking_ (take) every opportunity you get in life."
6. seem ___inf___ "Things aren't always what they seem _to be_ (be)."

2 Word builder Find out the meanings of these verbs, and write down the verb form(s) that can follow them. Then make up your own motto for each verb.

give up   promise   put off   refuse

Make a flip pad for the new verbs you have learned in this unit. Write each new verb in a sentence. Every time you have a spare minute, learn a verb!

 Now I can . . .

✔ I can . . .   ? I need to review how to . . .

- [ ] ask questions to get to know someone.
- [ ] tell interesting stories about my life.
- [ ] highlight key moments in a story.
- [ ] highlight important information in a story.

- [ ] understand a conversation about an accident.
- [ ] understand a podcast about an athlete's life story.
- [ ] read an article about a person who overcame an obstacle.
- [ ] write an anecdote about facing a challenge.

Personal tastes

 Can Do! In this unit, you learn how to . . .

Lesson A
- Talk about fashion and makeovers
- Make comparisons with *(not) as . . . as*

Lesson B
- Ask negative questions when you expect someone to agree
- Describe clothing

Lesson C
- Show understanding by summarizing what people say
- Use *Now* to introduce follow-up questions

Lesson D
- Read an article about how to develop a personal style
- Write questions and answers for an interview about personal style

1

2

3

4

Before you begin . . .

What kind of . . .
- music do you like?
- clothes do you wear?
- hairstyle looks good on you?
- car would you like?

Do you and your classmates have similar tastes?

11

Would you let a friend give YOU a makeover?

before

We gave Cindy and Scott, two very good friends, the chance to choose a new look for each other. How did they do? Here's the verdict!

before

after

after

What do you think about your new look, Cindy?

I love it! I don't usually wear these colors, but this dress is really nice. I like it. I wouldn't usually wear this much makeup – I try to get ready as quickly as I can in the morning – but it looks good. I'm really pleased.

Scott, you chose a completely different look for Cindy. How do you like it?

I like it a lot. I tried as hard as I could to find a style that suits her personality better. Her hair looks great. I mean, I don't usually like short hair as much as long hair, but it looks good on her, I think. And I like the dress on her. She looks great.

How do you like your new look, Scott?

Well, I kind of like it. I'm not used to wearing pants like these, but they're just as comfortable as my jeans. And Cindy made a good choice with the suede jacket. It's cool. Yeah, I don't look as scruffy as I did!

Cindy, do you like Scott's new look? He looks very different!

Yes, I really like it. He doesn't pay as much attention to his appearance as he should. Actually, the pastel shirt I chose doesn't look as good on him as the bright colors he usually wears. I don't think I like pastels that much, after all. But overall, he looks a lot better! I like his hair short like that.

1 Getting started

A Look at the "before" and "after" pictures of Cindy and Scott. What has changed?

B ◀)) 1.11 Listen. What do Cindy and Scott think about their makeovers? Do you agree with their comments?

Figure it out **C** How do Cindy and Scott actually say these things? Find the sentences in the article above. Compare with a partner.

1. **Scott** These pants and my jeans are equally comfortable.
2. **Scott** I used to look scruffier.
3. **Cindy** He should pay more attention to his appearance.
4. **Cindy** I try to get ready quickly in the morning – I can't get ready faster.

2 Grammar Comparisons with *(not) as . . . as* 🔊 1.12

Extra practice p. 141

You can make comparisons with *(not) as . . . as* with adjectives, nouns, and adverbs.

Adjectives The pants are just **as comfortable as** my jeans. (They're the same.)
The pants are **not as comfortable as** my jeans. (They're less comfortable.)
I **don't** look **as scruffy as** I did. (I was scruffier before.)

Nouns She spends **as little time as** possible on her makeup.
She **doesn't** wear **as many bright colors as** she should.
He **doesn't** pay **as much attention** to his appearance **as** he should.

Adverbs I tried **as hard as** I could to find the right style for her.
I **don't** like short hair **as much as** long hair.

> ✖ **Common errors**
>
> Don't forget the first *as*.
>
> Jeans aren't ***as*** nice as pants.
> (NOT Jeans ~~aren't nice as~~ pants.)

A Complete the sentences. Use the words in parentheses and *as . . . as*.

1. Older people ___*don't care as much as*___ (not care / much) younger
   people about their appearance.
2. Makeover shows _____*aren't* ^as *interesting as*_____ (not be / interesting) other
   ✓ reality shows on TV.
3. Men __*spend   as much*_____ (spend / much) money on themselves
   __*as*____ women do.
4. When I choose clothes, looks *are as important as*_____
   (be / important) comfort.
5. I _*don't have* ^as *many*_____ (not have / many) clothes and
   shoes _*as*_____ I'd like.
6. I _*spend   as little time as*_ (spend / little time) possible shopping for
   clothes.
7. Today's styles _*aren't as attractive as*_ (not be / attractive) the styles of ten years ago.
8. Women _*gets haircuts as often as*_ (get haircuts / often) men.

About you **B Pair work** Do you agree with the statements above? Explain your views.

3 Speaking naturally Linking words with the same consonant sound

big glasses	*wear red*	*dark colors*	*some makeup*	*stylish shoes*

A 🔊 1.13 **Listen and repeat the expressions above. Notice that when the same consonant sound is at
the end of one word and at the start of the next, it is pronounced once, but it sounds longer.**

About you **B** 🔊 1.14 **Now listen and repeat these statements. Are they true for you? Discuss with a partner.**

1. I think men loo**k c**ool in shirts and ties.
2. I don't like bi**g g**lasses. They're le**ss s**tylish than small glasses.
3. I li**ke c**asual clothes. I can't stan**d d**ressing up for anything.
4. I think women should always wear so**me m**akeup.
5. I own a lot of bla**ck c**lothes. I ha**te t**o wear bright colors, and I never wea**r r**ed.
6. There are a lot of styli**sh sh**ops in my neighborhood. They sell some goo**d d**esigner stuff.

1 Building language

A 🔊 **1.15** Listen. Why doesn't Ben like the jacket? Practice the conversation.

Yoko   Oh, don't you just love this jacket? I mean, isn't it great?

Ben   Hmm. I don't know.

Yoko   Don't you like it? I think it's really nice.

Ben   It's OK. It's kind of bright.

Yoko   But don't you like the style? It'd look good on you, don't you think?

Ben   Well, maybe.

Yoko   Well, don't you want to try it on, at least?

Ben   Not really. And anyway, isn't it a little expensive?

Yoko   Oh, isn't it on sale?

Ben   No. It's full price. The sale rack is over there. Hey, look at those jackets. Aren't they great?

Figure it out   **B**   How does Yoko actually say these things? Underline what she says in the conversation.

1. I love this jacket!   2. I think you should try it on.   3. I'm surprised you don't like it.

2 Grammar   Negative questions 🔊 1.16

Extra practice p. 141

When you want or expect someone to agree with you, you can use negative questions.

To express an opinion	To suggest an idea	To show surprise
Isn't this jacket great?	**Aren't** they a little expensive?	**Isn't** it on sale?
Don't you think it's great?	**Don't** you think it's too bright?	**Don't** you like it?
Doesn't that look good on him?	It'd look good, **don't** you think?	**Doesn't** she like it?

Look at the rest of Yoko and Ben's conversation. Rewrite the underlined sentences as negative questions. Then practice with a partner.

Ben   Look at these jackets. I think they're nice.

Yoko   Well, I'm not sure about the color. They're kind of plain.

Ben   Really? I'm surprised you don't like them. Look. This one looks good.

Yoko   Um . . . it's a little tight. It looks kind of small.

Ben   No, it's just right. I think I'll get it!

Yoko   *And* it's not as cheap as the other jackets.

Ben   Oh, it's not the same price. Well, maybe we should look around a bit more.

Aren't they nice? / Don't you think they're nice?

3 Building vocabulary

A Pair work Read the product descriptions on the website. What do you think about each item?

"Those rubber boots are cool." *"Aren't they a bit bright?"*

EASY SHOPPING

| OUTERWEAR |
| SHIRTS |
| PANTS |
| FOOTWEAR |
| ACCESSORIES |
| ACTIVEWEAR |
| KIDS |
| GIFT CARDS |
| **FREE SHIPPING OVER $50** |

1 Choose from our huge selection of men's and women's **leather** and **suede** jackets.

2 Luxury **cashmere** scarves and **silk** ties make perfect gifts.

3 Men's **wool** **turtleneck** and **V-neck** sweaters will keep you warm all winter.

4 Women's **long-sleeved cotton** tops are available in a range of **solid colors**. Shown here in **neon** green, **dark** green, and **light** green.

5 Looking for **denim** jeans? Whether you want **boot-cut** or **flared, fitted, skinny,** or **baggy** – we have jeans to fit you!

6 Women's **short-sleeved striped** shirts in **polyester**. **Floral-print** and **plaid** shirts also available.

7 Our **rubber** boots come in a variety of patterns. Shown here in **turquoise** with a **polka-dot** pattern.

B Complete the chart with the words in bold above, and add your own ideas. Then compare with a partner. Do any of these words describe clothes that you and your classmates are wearing?

Word sort

Colors	Patterns	Materials		Styles	
neon green	striped	leather	Denim	V-neck	fitted
Dark green	Floral-print	Suede	striped	Turtleneck	Skinny
Light green	Plaid	Cashmere	Polyester	Long-sleeved	Baggy
Photos solid colors	Polka-dot	Silk	Rubber boots	Boot-cut	Short-sleeved
Turquoise	Stripped	Cotton	Wool	flored	

> **Vocabulary notebook** p. 20

4 Talk about it Different styles

Group work Discuss the following questions. Use negative questions where possible.

▸ What styles are in fashion right now? What colors? What fabrics? Do you like them?

▸ What kinds of styles look good on you? How about your friends?

▸ What colors are the clothes in your closet? What materials are they made of?

▸ Are there any colors you won't wear? Why?

▸ Would you buy any of the items on the website above? Why? Why not?

"Well, skinny jeans are in fashion, but don't you think they look kind of ugly?"

> **Sounds right** p. 137

1 Conversation strategy Summarizing things people say

A Pair work Who do you buy gifts for?
What do you usually buy? Tell the class.

B 🔊 1.17 **Listen. What do you find out about Don's sister?**

Janet	What do you want to get for your sister? What kind of things does she like?
Don	Well, she likes to read. She likes music. She likes to cook, sew . . .
Janet	She seems to have a lot of different interests.
Don	Yeah. I'm not sure what to get her. She has hundreds of books already.
Janet	She has a big collection, then.
Don	Yeah. And she has a ton of music and as much stuff for the kitchen as she could ever want.
Janet	Sounds like she has everything she needs.
Don	Yeah. She doesn't really need anything.
Janet	Now, doesn't she travel a lot? Because you could get her an e-reader or a tablet or something.
Don	Actually, that's a great idea. She's always complaining about carrying her books everywhere. I think I'll do that.

C Notice how Janet summarizes the things Don says. It shows she's involved in the conversation and is following what Don is saying. Find more examples.

"She seems to have a lot of different interests."

D Match each statement with the best response. Write the letters a to g. Then practice with a partner.

1. I only download free books or go to the library. _g_
2. I've downloaded thousands of songs. _f_
3. A friend of mine never seems to like the gifts I give her. _e_
4. It's hard to buy gifts for my dad. He never wants anything. _b_
5. My mom reads a lot. She knows everything. _a_
6. My boyfriend remembers the lyrics of every song he hears. _c_
7. I read all kinds of stuff, from romance to science fiction. _d_

a. Sounds like she's a walking encyclopedia.
b. Yeah. What do you buy the man who has everything?
c. Wow. He has a fantastic memory.
d. Gosh. You have really broad tastes.
e. Sounds like she's really choosy.
f. You have a huge collection, then.
g. Right. You don't buy books, then.

2 Strategy plus *Now*

Now is often used to introduce a follow-up question. It shows that you want to move the conversation on to a different aspect of a topic.

 In conversation

Now is one of the top 100 words. About 20% of the uses of *now* are to introduce questions.

She doesn't really need anything.

Now, doesn't she travel a lot?

Find two follow-up questions for each conversation. Write the letters *a* to *f*. Then practice with a partner. Ask the questions again and give your own answers.

a. Now, do you have an idea before you start looking?	d. Now, do you have similar tastes?
b. Now, do you like to do all the tourist things?	e. Now, do you usually go alone?
c. Now, does she have a background in design?	f. Now, do you ask what people want?

1. A Do you like to shop for gifts?

   B Yeah. I like to look for something really unusual. You know, something different.

   A So you put some thought into it. __a__ __d__

2. A So, are you good at decorating your home? Like choosing colors and fabrics?

   B No, not at all! My wife does all that stuff. She loves buying cushions and things like that.

   A So you're not interested in that. __c__ __f__

3. A So, I heard you like to travel a lot?

   B Yeah, I really like going to a new city and seeing the sights.

   A So you like exploring. __b__ __e__

3 Listening and strategies Broad tastes

A 🔊 1.18 Listen to three conversations. Who has broad tastes? Write the name or names. Then listen again and answer the questions below.

1. What happens in the cooking show? How did Mary learn to cook?
2. What is Nick listening to? How did Nick get into that kind of music?
3. Why is James exhausted? How did James get into sci-fi?

B 🔊 1.19 Now listen to three excerpts from the conversations. Circle the best response.

1. a. So you don't do it much anymore.   b. Wow. You know what you're doing.
2. a. Really? You play everything.   b. So you gave it up.
3. a. You think anything's possible, then.   b. Right. It doesn't seem real at all.

About you **C Pair work** What kind of tastes do you have in movies, food, and music? Discuss with a partner.

A *I love classic movies. I think they're just as good as the movies they make these days.*

B *Really? So you're into old movies. Now, what genres do you like? Sci-fi or . . . ?*

1 Reading

A Can you think of some ways to dress well without spending a lot of money? Tell the class.

B Read the article. Does it mention any of your ideas?
Which ideas are the best? Which ideas have you tried?

> **Reading tip**
>
> Read the first sentence of each tip to see what the article covers.

HOW TO DEVELOP YOUR PERSONAL STYLE

Do you ever worry that you don't look as great as you could? Maybe you don't have as much time – or money – as you'd like to spend on yourself. But dressing well is important because knowing you look good makes you feel more confident.

Developing your own personal style is not as hard (or as expensive) as you might think! Even jeans and a T-shirt can look as stylish as a dressy outfit – if you know how to put them together. Here are some quick, inexpensive tips to help you create your own fabulous personal style.

❶ Don't wear clothes that are too "old" or too "young" for you, and choose styles that are appropriate for your lifestyle. _____ You want to feel as comfortable as possible.

❷ Flip through a magazine to find styles you like. Use the photos as a guide. _____

❸ Look at photos of yourself wearing a variety of outfits. Which ones look good on you? Which ones aren't particularly flattering? Notice what you like and dislike about different outfits. Is it the fabric? The color? The style?

❹ Think about your life goals. Are you looking for a job? To impress potential employers, liven up your professional look by adding some accessories to the suit you already have. How about a scarf? A colorful new tie?

❺ Call attention to your best features. Choose colors that bring out the color of your eyes. _____ If you're not as slim as you'd like to be, buy tailored clothes that fit well. Don't just wear baggy outfits to cover up those few extra pounds. Choose the best fabrics for your shape. Silk may feel nice, but be careful – shiny fabrics can make you look heavier. Cashmere, on the other hand, can make you look slimmer and looks especially good on muscular men.

❻ Clean out your closet. _____ Get rid of stained, out of shape, torn, faded, or out-of-style clothing and scuffed shoes. Sell them at a consignment store, and use the extra cash to jazz up your wardrobe.

❼ Update an outfit you already have. Add a new belt. If your jeans are worn at the bottom, cut them off to make a pair of capris.

❽ Make sure you have a few essentials. Men need a well-fitting sweater with a pair of casual but well-cut pants. For women, a classic black dress and a pair of simple pants that you can dress up or down are must-haves. _____

C Where do these sentences fit in the article? Write the correct letters in the spaces.

a. If you want to look taller, wear clothes with vertical stripes.
b. Bring the pictures with you when you go shopping.
c. And for both men and women, a pair of classic black shoes is a necessity.
d. Take out everything that doesn't fit you anymore.
e. If you walk everywhere, be sure to buy shoes that are comfortable as well as stylish.

2 Listening and speaking Keeping up with trends

A 🔊 1.20 Listen to four people talk about trends. Number the topics 1 to 4.
There is one extra topic.

| 3 hairstyles | 1 fashion | 2 technology | ☐ cars | 4 sports and fitness ✓ |

B 🔊 1.20 Listen again. Do the people keep up with trends? Circle *Yes* or *No*. Write one thing they do or don't do.

	Keeps up with trends?	What do they do or not do?
1. Maddy	Yes / **No**	She doesn't care about trends, she don't have too thing's
2. Frank	**Yes** / No	Waiting line for hours for buying thing's in the first day
3. Laura	**Yes** / No	Try new thing's. Her stylish is very creative and she does to
4. Nate	Yes / **No**	Not as fit as posible, not muscular.

About you **C** Pair work What are the current trends in each area in Exercise A? Do you keep up with the trends? Why? Why not?

3 Writing Style interview

A Read the question and answer below and the Help note. Add commas (,) where needed and a dash (–), and change one period to an exclamation mark (!).

How would you describe your tastes in clothes?

I like to wear fashionable clothes when I go out with my friends. I get ideas from men's clothing stores magazines and from my friends. At home I like to wear something more comfortable my old jeans a T-shirt and sneakers. I look completely different.

> **Help note**
>
> **Punctuation**
> • Use commas (,) in lists.
>   *My clothes are fun, colorful, and unusual.*
> • Use a dash (–) to add or explain more about something.
> • Use an exclamation mark (!) for emphasis.
>   *I wear every color under the sun – sometimes all at once!*

About you **B** Write three questions about personal style. Then exchange papers with a partner. Write answers to your partner's questions.

C Pair work Read your partner's answers to your questions. Check the punctuation.

Free talk p. 129

Vocabulary notebook / Blue suede shoes

Learning tip *Labeling pictures*

When you want to learn a new set of vocabulary, find and label pictures illustrating the new words. For example, you can use a fashion magazine to label items of clothing, styles, colors, patterns, and materials.

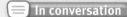
1 What styles of clothing, colors, and patterns can you see in the picture? What materials do you think the clothes are made of? Label the picture with words from the box and other words you know.

✓baggy	✓polka-dot
dark brown	short-sleeved
fitted / skinny	silk
flared	striped
floral-print	✓suede
leather	turquoise
✓light blue	✓turtleneck
long-sleeved	✓V-neck
neon orange	wool

Light blue polka dot dress

V neck short sleeved T shirt

Bell-bottom Flared jeans

baggy

suede

skinny Floral-print pants

2 **Word builder** Find out what these words mean. Then find an example of each one in the picture above, and add labels.

ankle-length	gold	navy blue
beige	maroon	plastic
crew-neck	mauve	tweed

On your own

Find a fashion magazine and label as many of the different styles, materials, patterns, and colors as you can in ten minutes.

✓ Can Do! Now I can . . .

✓ I can . . .	? I need to review how to . . .

☐ talk about my tastes in clothes and fashion.

☐ compare how people look different over time.

☐ describe patterns, materials, and styles of clothing.

☐ show I understand by summarizing what people say.

☐ use *Now* to introduce follow-up questions.

☐ understand conversations about food, music, and movies.

☐ understand people discussing trends.

☐ read an article about how to develop a personal style.

☐ write interview questions and answers.

World cultures

☑ Can Do! In this unit, you learn how to . . .

Lesson A
- Talk about your culture using the simple present passive

Lesson B
- Talk about customs and manners using verb + -ing and to + verb

Lesson C
- Use expressions like *to be honest* to sound more direct
- Use *of course* to give information that is not surprising, or to agree

Lesson D
- Read an article about proverbs
- Write an article about a favorite proverb

1   2   3

4   5   6

Before you begin . . .

What are some of the cultural traditions in your country? Think of a typical . . .

- dish or drink.
- type of music or dance.
- symbol.
- festival.
- item of clothing.
- handicraft.

21

What not to miss . . .

WE ASKED PEOPLE:
What's one thing you shouldn't miss on a visit to . . . ?

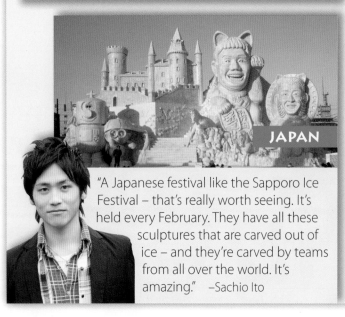

SOUTH KOREA

"Oh, Korean food! We have so many different dishes. One typical dish is *kimbap*. It's made with rice and vegetables and wrapped in dried seaweed. And it's eaten cold. It's delicious." –Min-hee Park

PERU

"Well, Peru has some beautiful handicrafts. A lot of them are exported nowadays, and they're sold all over the world. But it's still worth visiting a local market. These earrings are made locally. They're made of silver."
–Elena Camacho

JAPAN

"A Japanese festival like the Sapporo Ice Festival – that's really worth seeing. It's held every February. They have all these sculptures that are carved out of ice – and they're carved by teams from all over the world. It's amazing."   –Sachio Ito

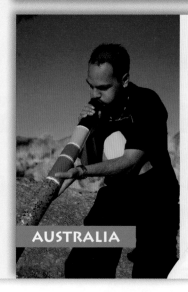

"Oh, you should go to a performance of traditional Aboriginal music. They play this instrument – it's called a *didgeridoo*. It's made out of a hollow piece of wood and painted by hand. It makes a really interesting sound."
–Robert Flynn

AUSTRALIA

1 Getting started

A Look at the countries above. What do you know about each country? Make a list of ideas.

B 🔊 1.21 Listen. What aspect of their country's culture does each person talk about?

C Rewrite the sentences below, but keep the same meaning. Use the comments above to help you.

1. You eat *kimbap* cold.   *Kimbap* <u>is eaten</u> cold.
2. People make earrings like these locally.   Earrings like these <u>are made</u> locally.
3. They export a lot of handicrafts.   A lot of handicrafts <u>are exported</u>.
4. Teams from all over the world carve   The sculptures <u>are carved</u> by teams
   the sculptures.   from all over the world.

2 Grammar The simple present passive ◄)) 1.22

Extra practice p. 142

Use the passive when the "doer" of the action is not known or not important.

Active	Passive
How do they make *kimbap*?	How **is** *kimbap* **made**?
They make it with rice and vegetables.	It**'s made** with rice and vegetables.
Do they eat it hot or cold?	**Is** it **eaten** hot or cold?
They eat it cold. They don't eat it hot.	It**'s eaten** cold. It**'s** not **eaten** hot.
They carve the sculptures out of ice.	The sculptures **are carved** out of ice.

> **In conversation**
>
> The most common passive verbs are *made*, *done*, and *called*.

If the "doer" of the action is important, you can introduce it with *by*.

The sculptures **are carved by** teams from all over the world.

> ✖ **Common errors**
>
> Be sure to use the verb *be* in the present simple passive.
>
> The sculptures **are** carved out of ice. (NOT ~~The sculptures carved out of ice.~~)

About you **A** **Rewrite the questions about your country. Then write true answers. Use the simple present passive.**

1. When do people sing the national anthem?
   When is the national anthem sung? It's sung . . .
2. How do you make your favorite traditional food? Do you serve it cold?
3. Do both men and women play your country's national sports?
4. When do people celebrate your most important festivals? Does everybody celebrate them?
5. When do people wear the national costume? Do people wear it a lot?
6. Do people play traditional folk music?
7. Do people make traditional handicrafts? Where do they sell them?

About you **B** **Pair work** Compare your answers with a partner. Can you add more ideas?

3 Speaking naturally Silent syllables

ev~~e~~ry	diff~~e~~rent	int~~e~~resting	veg~~e~~table

A ◄)) 1.23 Listen and repeat the words. Notice that the unstressed vowels are not pronounced.

B ◄)) 1.24 Listen to people talk about their cities. Cross out the vowel that is not pronounced in the underlined words. Then read the sentences to a partner.

1. Broc, Switzerland: We're known for our choc~~o~~late, which is sold all over the world. If you're really interested, you can visit a factory to learn about the hist~~o~~ry of choc~~o~~late and how it's made.
2. Coober Pedy, Australia: The av~~e~~rage temp~~e~~rature here in summer is almost 40°C, so it's much cooler to live underground. It's definitely something diff~~e~~rent for travelers!
3. Akihabara, Japan: If you want a cam~~e~~ra, then you have to shop here. Practic~~a~~lly ev~~e~~ry brand of electronic and computer goods is displayed here!
4. Boyacá, Colombia: Em~~e~~ralds are mined all over the world, but our region has some of the best and most valu~~a~~ble stones. They're mostly exported and made into jew~~e~~lry.

About you **C** **Choose a city, region, or country, and tell the class what it's known for. Guess the places your classmates talk about.**

"This place is known for its wooden dolls. They're painted by local artists."

1 Building vocabulary and grammar

A 🔊 **1.25** Listen. Are these statements true in your country? Check (✓) True or False.

		True	False
1.	Eating food on a subway or bus is bad manners.	☒	☐
2.	It's rude to **cut in line**.	☒	☐
3.	You should try to **keep your voice down** in public.	☒	☐
4.	You can offend someone by not **bowing** or **shaking hands** when you meet.	☒	☒
5.	People might **stare** at you for **walking around barefoot**.	☐	☐
6.	**Having an argument** in public is considered bad manners.	☒	☐
7.	It's impolite to walk into someone's home without **taking off your shoes**.	☐	☒
8.	**Showing affection** in public – **holding hands** or **kissing** – is inappropriate.	☐	☒
9.	You should try not to **stand too close** to people. It's considered rude.	☐	☒
10.	It's acceptable not to **tip** cab drivers.	☒	☐
11.	You should be careful not to **point at people**.	☒	☐
12.	It's customary to **bargain** with street vendors to get something cheaper, but it's not acceptable to do this in a store.	☒	☐

Word sort **B** What behaviors are considered acceptable in your country? Complete the chart with ideas from above. Add your own ideas. Then compare with a partner.

It's acceptable to . . .	It's not acceptable to . . .
take your shoes off in the house.	*stand too close to people.*

Figure it out **C** Circle the correct choices. Are the sentences true in your country? Discuss with a partner.

Vocabulary notebook p. 30

1. **Cut / Cutting** in line is bad manners.
2. You might offend someone by **standing / stand** too close.
3. You can offend your host by not **taking / to take** off your shoes.
4. It's polite **bow / to bow** when you meet someone.
5. It's customary not **to tip / tip** cab drivers.

2 Grammar Verb + *-ing* and *to* + verb; position of *not* ◄)) 1.26

Extra practice p. 142

Verb + *-ing* as a subject
Eating in public is bad manners.
Not shaking hands is impolite.

Verb + *-ing* after prepositions
You can offend people by **eating** in public.
People might stare at you for **not shaking** hands.

***to* + verb after *It's* . . .**
It's bad manners **to eat** in public.
It's impolite **not to shake** hands.

Position of *not*
***Not* comes before the word it negates.**
Be careful **not** to point at people.
You can offend people by **not** bowing.

Notice the difference in meaning:
It's acceptable **not** to tip cab drivers.
(It's optional.)
It's **not** acceptable to tip cab drivers.
(You shouldn't do it.)

A Complete the sentences about eating at restaurants. Use verb + *-ing* or *to* + verb.

1. If a friend invites you out to dinner, it's inappropriate _to take_ (take) another friend with you.

2. It's bad manners _not to call_ (not /call) the restaurant if you have a reservation and you decide to cancel your plans.

3. _Arriving_ (arrive) a little late when you meet a big group of friends at a restaurant is acceptable. _Not showing_ (not / show) up at all is impolite.

4. If you get to the restaurant before your friend, it's fine _to sit_ (sit) down at the table.

5. It's not acceptable _to complain_ (complain) to your server if you don't like your meal.

6. People might be upset with you for _not paying_ (not / pay) your fair share of the bill.

7. _Talking_ (talk) with your mouth full is considered rude. _Taking_ (take) phone calls during dinner is also bad manners.

8. You can offend the server by _not leaving_ (not / leave) a tip. But _giving_ (give) a smaller tip is fine if the service is bad.

9. _Asking_ (ask) the server for a box to bring your leftover food home is acceptable.

10. It's bad manners _not thank_ (not thank) the person who paid afterwards. _Not saying_ (not say) thank you is really impolite.

About you **B** Pair work Discuss the statements above. Which ones do you agree with? Can you add more etiquette advice?

A Yeah. Taking another friend with you is rude – especially if you're not paying.
B But it's not rude to invite another friend if it's a casual evening out.

About you **C** Pair work What etiquette advice can you think of for the following situations? Make a list and then share with another pair.

visiting someone's home   going to a birthday party   going to an interview

"Well, when you visit someone's home, you might offend the host by not bringing a gift."

(((**Sounds right** p. 137

1 Conversation strategy Sounding more direct

A What kinds of things do people miss about home when they move abroad? Make a list.

B 🔊 1.27 Listen. What would David miss if he left Brazil?

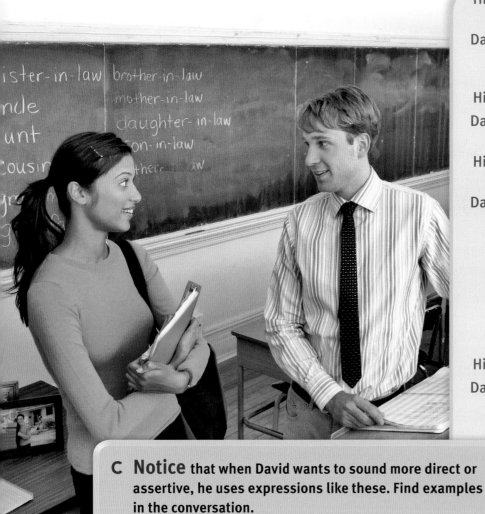

Hilda	So, when you're living here, do you miss home?
David	Um, I don't miss too much, to be honest. Um, I miss my family, of course. . . .
Hilda	Right.
David	But I definitely don't miss the food! Um, I miss my family. That's about it.
Hilda	So, if you went back home, would you miss lots of things about Brazil?
David	Oh, yeah. I'd absolutely miss the food here. Yeah. But actually, I think the biggest thing would be . . . it would be weird for me to live in a country where I knew the language already, where all I have to do is work. I just don't see a challenge in that. You know, here every day is a challenge, speaking the language.
Hilda	Uh-huh.
David	In fact, living back home would be boring, I think. I honestly don't know what I'd do.

C **Notice** that when David wants to sound more direct or assertive, he uses expressions like these. Find examples in the conversation.

absolutely, definitely, really, actually, certainly, honestly, in fact, to be honest, to tell you the truth

About you **D** Make these statements about living in another country more direct. Use the expressions given. Then discuss each statement with a partner. Do you agree?

1. I'd miss my friends. (definitely) I'd miss everyone. (in fact)
2. I wouldn't miss the weather. (certainly) But I'd miss the food. (really)
3. I'd enjoy living in a different culture. (actually)
4. Learning the language would be a challenge. (to be honest)
5. I wouldn't miss the lifestyle here. (to tell you the truth)
6. I think I'd be scared to go abroad on my own. (honestly)

    A *If I lived in another country, I'd definitely miss my friends!*
    B *Well, yes, but to be honest, it's good to make new friends too.*

2 Strategy plus *of course*

Of course usually means, "This idea is not surprising. It's what you expect."

You can also use *Of course* in responses to show you agree or understand.

A I really miss my family.
B Of course.

> I miss my family, of course.

i Note

Be careful when you use *of course*. It can sound abrupt or rude as an answer to a question.

A Do you miss your family?
B Oh, yes, I really do.
(NOT ~~Of course.~~)

In conversation

Of course is one of the top 50 expressions.

A Read the conversations. Which response is more polite? Circle *a* or *b*.

1. Do you think living in another country would be exciting?
   a. Of course it would.
   b. Absolutely. Of course, I'd probably feel homesick at times.

2. Would you learn all about a country before you went?
   a. Well, I guess I'd like to know all about its culture. And, of course, its traditions.
   b. But of course. You really should learn something.

3. Would you take something with you to remind you of home?
   a. Of course.
   b. Probably. Maybe a photo of my cat. Of course, I couldn't take the cat with me, but . . .

About you **B** **Pair work** Ask and answer the questions above, giving your own answers. Use *of course* in your answers, but be careful how you use it.

3 Listening and strategies Away from home

A ◀))) 1.28 Listen to Val talk about her experience. Answer the questions.

1. Why is she living away from home?
2. What has been challenging for her?
3. What has been going well?
4. How does she keep in touch with family? When?

B ◀))) 1.28 Listen again. What would Val's friend say about her experience? Check (✓) the sentences.

1. ☐ T To tell you the truth, Val's host sister is pretty unfriendly.
2. ☐ F To be honest, she hasn't gotten to know many people.
3. ☐ T She's definitely learning about the culture.
4. ☐ T Of course, she doesn't like having to be home at ten.
5. ☐ F She's certainly homesick. In fact, she wants to go back home right now.

About you **C** **Group work** Think about a time you were away from home. Who and what did you miss? How did you keep in touch? Talk about your experience.

"When I was an exchange student, I missed my friends. Of course, I missed my family, too."

1 Reading

A Think of a proverb in your language. When is it used, and why?

B Read the article. Do you have similar proverbs in your language? Are proverbs used in the same ways?

> **Reading tip**
> Read the first sentence of each paragraph. What do you think each paragraph will be about?

PROVERBS: The wisdom that binds us together

Proverbs exist in every language and culture and are a way of passing down folk wisdom, or "common sense," from generation to generation. Who doesn't remember a time when they were struggling with a problem or dilemma, and someone quoted a proverb that aptly summed up or explained the situation? "All's fair in love and war" describes the injustice that is often encountered in a romantic relationship and may help some of us accept it. "Absence makes the heart grow fonder" is meant to give hope when a loved one is far away. When that same relationship is brought to an end by distance, we hear, "Out of sight, out of mind."

Proverbs have lasted for thousands of years, probably because they're so memorable. Some are short and concise, like "Practice makes perfect" and "Haste makes waste," while others use a poetic language such as metaphors, repetition, and rhymes. The metaphor "Out of the frying pan and into the fire" is easy to visualize when you are faced with a difficult situation that just got even worse. The repetition of the consonant "t" makes it easy to remember "It takes two to tango." The rhyme "When the cat's away, the mice will play" comes to mind as soon as the boss leaves on vacation, and the repetition of the structure in "Once bitten, twice shy" makes this an extremely catchy phrase.

Some scholars who study proverbs look for examples that are unique to a particular culture as a key to understanding cultural differences. Others focus on the proverbs that appear in almost every language as a way of defining a common wisdom that binds all humans together.

Proverbs don't always offer up universal truth, however, and they are frequently contradictory. People say, "Clothes make the man," to reflect the importance of appearance as part of one's personal identity. On the other hand, they also say, "You can't judge a book by its cover," to point out that appearances can be deceptive. And with "Handsome is as handsome does" they stress the value of good behavior over good looks.

So while proverbs can help us grasp some universally shared wisdom, they also force us to recognize that life is complex and that there are no easy answers. The complexity of the human condition as reflected in proverbs is yet another thing that is shared by people around the world.

C Read the article again. Can you find these things? Compare with a partner.

1. a function proverbs serve in different languages and cultures
2. two different ways scholars look at proverbs
3. two proverbs that are memorable because they use rhyme
4. three proverbs that are memorable because they repeat consonants, words, or structures
5. two pairs of proverbs that are contradictory
6. two things we can learn when we study proverbs from different cultures

Listening and speaking Favorite proverbs

A Can you guess the meaning of the proverbs below? Discuss with a partner.

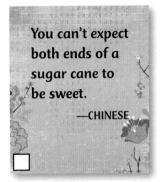

B ◀)) **1.29** Listen to four people talk about their favorite proverbs. Number the proverbs above 1 to 4. What do they mean? Did you guess the meaning correctly?

C ◀)) **1.30** Match each proverb above with a similar English proverb below. Write the numbers. Then listen again as someone comments on each proverb, and check your answers.

a. You can't have your cake and eat it, too. _____

b. Every cloud has a silver lining. _____

c. If you can't stand the heat, get out of the kitchen. _____

d. Beggars can't be choosers. _____

About you **D** **Pair work** Which of the proverbs above is your favorite? Why? When would you use it?

"'Beggars can't be choosers' is used a lot in our house. My mom is always saying it. It's great because . . ."

 Writing Explain a proverb

A Read the article below. Find the useful expressions from the Help note, and underline them.

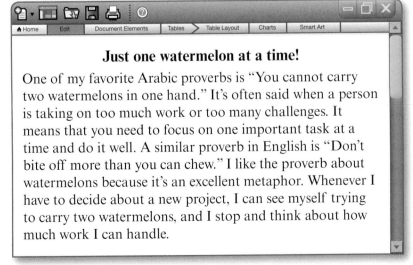

Just one watermelon at a time!

One of my favorite Arabic proverbs is "You cannot carry two watermelons in one hand." It's often said when a person is taking on too much work or too many challenges. It means that you need to focus on one important task at a time and do it well. A similar proverb in English is "Don't bite off more than you can chew." I like the proverb about watermelons because it's an excellent metaphor. Whenever I have to decide about a new project, I can see myself trying to carry two watermelons, and I stop and think about how much work I can handle.

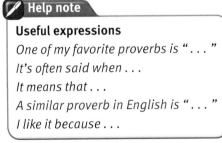

Help note

Useful expressions

One of my favorite proverbs is " . . . "

It's often said when . . .

It means that . . .

A similar proverb in English is " . . . "

I like it because . . .

B Write a short article about your favorite proverb. Say why you like it and what it means. Then read your classmates' articles. Did anyone choose the same proverb?

Free talk p. 130

Vocabulary notebook / Travel etiquette

Learning tip *Finding examples*

When you learn a new expression, find examples on the Internet. Type the expressions into an Internet search engine with quotation marks (" ") around it.

1 **Complete the sentences using the words and expressions in the box.**

bowing	having an argument	kissing	to take off	walking around barefoot
eating	to keep your voice down	to cut in line	to shake hands	

1. In Japan, _____ is customary when two people introduce themselves.
2. In the United States, it's polite _____ firmly when you are introduced to a colleague.
3. In South Korea, _____ food on the subway is considered rude.
4. In many places of worship in Asia, it's polite _____ your hat and shoes.
5. In Chile, people often say hello by _____ each other on the cheek.
6. In Australia, _____ is acceptable at beach resorts, but not in public buildings.
7. In Taiwan, _____ in public is considered impolite. It's better _____ .
8. In Great Britain, it's considered rude _____ . You should always wait your turn.

2 **Word builder** **Find the meaning of the words and expressions. Write a tip for each one.**

blow your nose	burp	offer your seat to someone	swear

 ### On your own

Find a travel guide for a country you'd like to visit. Find six things you should or shouldn't do if you go there.

Be prepared for a kiss on the cheek.

VISITOR'S GUIDE TO CHILE

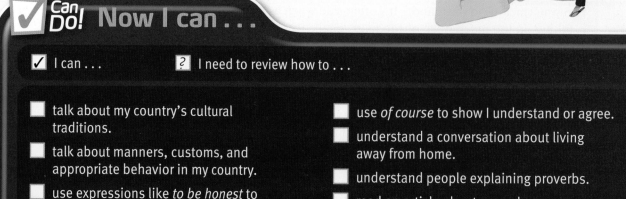

✓ Can Do! Now I can . . .

✓ I can . . .   ❓ I need to review how to . . .

☐ talk about my country's cultural traditions.

☐ talk about manners, customs, and appropriate behavior in my country.

☐ use expressions like *to be honest* to sound more direct.

☐ use *of course* to show I understand or agree.

☐ understand a conversation about living away from home.

☐ understand people explaining proverbs.

☐ read an article about proverbs.

☐ write an article about a favorite proverb.

To be + V.ing

1 Is it polite?

A Complete the questions with the correct forms of the verbs.

1. Would you ever consider ___not tipping___ (not tip) a server in a restaurant?
2. Do you remember _staring_ (stare) at people when you were little?
3. Do you feel it's rude _not to say_ (not say) hello to your neighbors?
4. Is _the holding hands_ (hold hands) OK on a first date? x
5. Do you bother _to bargain_ (bargain) with street vendors when the items are already very cheap?
6. Do you ever offer _to help_ (help) people with their bags on the bus or subway? ✓
7. Have you and a friend ever ended up _arguing_ (argue) in public? ✓
8. Have you ever offended someone without _intending_ (intend) _to be_ (be) rude?

B Pair work Ask and answer the questions. Show that you understand your partner's answers by summarizing what he or she says.

"I'd never consider not tipping – I used to be a server myself."   *"So you always tip the server."*

2 Think, Bob, think!

A Complete the conversation with the correct forms of the verbs.

Officer ___Have___ you ___seen___ (see) these people before?

Bob Yes, they're my neighbors. They _live_ (live) upstairs.

Officer How long _have_ they _been living_ (live) there?

Bob I guess I _'ve known_ (know) them for six months.
They _'ve moved_ (move) here in August.

Officer When _did_ you last _see_ (see) them?

Bob Um, about a week ago, I think. Last Tuesday.

Officer What _were_ they _doing_ (do) when you
saw (see) them?

Bob Well, as I _was coming_ (come) home, they
were carrying (carry) a big suitcase to the car.

Officer _Did_ you _speak_ (speak) to them?

Bob I _said_ (say), "Hi! Where _did are_ you
going (go)?" And they _replied_ (reply),
"On vacation."

Officer What time _did_ they finally _leave_ (leave)?

Bob Oh, um, it was pretty late, around 11 at night, I guess.

Officer Can you remember what they _were wearing_ (wear)?

Bob Let me think. . . .

B Write Bob's answer to the police officer's last question. How much detail can you give? Compare with a partner.

3 Can you complete this conversation?

A Complete the conversation with the words and expressions in the box. Practice the conversation.

| ✓definitely   don't you think   now   of course   these   this   to be honest |

Anna Bella used to live in Japan. You loved living there, right?

Bella Oh, _____definitely_____ . I lived there for nine years, working for a Japanese advertising company.

Chris Nine years? Wow! Didn't you ever get homesick?

Bella Occasionally. But, _to be honest_ , I didn't really miss living at home. I was too busy. I mean, _of course_ I missed my family.

Chris Oh, I bet you did. _now_ , how did you get that job? Did they hire you over here, or . . . ?

Bella Actually, I was already in Japan on an exchange program, staying with _this_ family. And the father starts bringing home all _these_ documents from his work to translate into English. Anyway, I started helping him, and his company ended up hiring me.

Anna And they transferred her here. It's a cool story, _Don't you think_ ?

B **Pair work** Choose a topic below and have a conversation. Ask and answer questions.

- something difficult you did once
- an interesting experience you had
- a time you missed someone
- an unusual person you once met

  A Can you think of a time you missed someone?
  B Yes. My mom went on a trip when I was five. I wanted to go with her.

4 As bad as that?

Pair work Compare these things using *(not) as . . . as*. Try to use negative questions to give opinions or to suggest ideas.

- folk music / rock music
- baked potatoes / fries
- old buildings / new buildings
- cheap watches / expensive watches

A Folk music isn't as popular as rock music. You don't hear it as much.
B But don't you think it's just as good? I like folk as much as rock.

5 Guess the dish!

A Write questions in the simple present passive, using the words below. Then think of a traditional dish, and answer the questions.

1. eat / hot or cold
2. When / eat
3. How / cook
4. What / make / with
5. What / serve / with
6. What / call

B **Pair work** Take turns asking and answering the questions. Can you guess your partner's dish before question 6?

Socializing

✓ Can Do! In this unit, you learn how to . . .

Lesson A
- Say what should happen with *be supposed to*
- Talk about weekend plans using *was / were going to*

Lesson B
- Talk about going out and formal events using *get* expressions

Lesson C
- Check your understanding with "statement questions"
- Use *so* to start or close topics, pause, or check understanding

Lesson D
- Read an article about introverts and extroverts
- Write an article about your social style

1

2

3

4

Before you begin . . .

- Who do you usually socialize with?
- Do you usually go out in small groups, large groups, or with just one person?
- Where are some good places to go out with friends in your town or city?

Marco: Are you going to Brad and Gayle's party?

Anna: Well, I wasn't going to go, but maybe I will. I'm supposed to be studying for an exam. Are you going?

Marco: Yeah. The party's at their house, right? Do you know where they live?

Anna: Not exactly. Brad was going to call and give me the address, but he didn't. Maybe Ellen knows.

Ellen: What kind of party is it?

Phil: I think it's supposed to be a barbecue.

Ellen: That'll be fun. Have you heard the weather forecast?

Phil: Yeah. I heard it's supposed to be a really nice evening.

Anwar: Are we supposed to bring anything?

Sue: I don't think so. I was going to make some potato salad, but I didn't have time.

Anwar: Well, I bought them a box of chocolates. Do you think that'll be OK?

Sue: I don't know. Isn't Brad on a diet? He's not supposed to eat stuff like that. But Gayle will like them.

Patty: Jen and Martin are late. They were supposed to pick me up at 7:00.

Junko: Gosh, it's 7:30 already. Maybe they forgot. Do you want me to come and get you? I can take you home, too.

Patty: That'd be great. But I'm supposed to be at work early tomorrow, so I can't stay late.

Junko: That's OK. I think the party's supposed to end at 11:00, but we can leave a bit earlier.

1 Getting started

A What do you do to get ready for a party? Tell the class.

B 2.01 Listen. Brad and Gayle are having a party tonight, and their friends are getting ready. What do you find out about the party?

Figure it out **C** How might Brad and Gayle's friends say the things below? Replace the underlined words with an expression each person has already used above.

1. Phil They say it's going to be really warm.
2. Sue Brad shouldn't eat chocolate.
3. Patty I have to get up early tomorrow.
4. Anna I should be working on a paper.
5. Patty Jen and Martin agreed to be here by 7:00.
6. Sue I intended to make a dessert, but I didn't.

34

2 **Grammar** *be supposed to; was / were going to* ◀)) **2.02**

Extra practice p. 143

Be supposed to can mean "They say . . . ."	It**'s supposed to** be a barbecue. It**'s supposed to** rain later.
It can also mean "have to" or "should."	I**'m supposed to** work tomorrow. He**'s not supposed to** eat chocolate.
It can contrast what should happen with what does or will happen.	I**'m supposed to** be studying for an exam (but I'm not). I**'m not supposed to** stay out late (but maybe I will).
Was / Were supposed to can mean what was expected didn't or won't happen.	They **were supposed to** come at 7:00 (but they didn't). I **wasn't supposed to** go by myself (but I'll have to).
Was / Were going to has a similar meaning and can also mean "intended to."	He **was going to** give us directions (but he didn't). I **wasn't going to** go to the party (but I guess I will).

In conversation

Over 60% of uses of *be supposed to* are in the present tense. About 10% are negative.

Complete the conversations with the correct form of *be supposed to* or *was / were going to* and the verb. Sometimes more than one answer is possible. Then practice in pairs.

Common errors

Be sure to use the correct form of *be supposed to*.

I'm supposed to work tomorrow.
(NOT ~~I suppose to~~ work tomorrow.)

1. A   It's supposed to be raining (rain) tonight. Do you want to go see a movie?

    B   Yeah. I want to see that new Stephen King movie.
        It's supposed to be (be) good. I was supposed to see (see)
        it last weekend, but I ended up going to a party instead.

2. A   Do you have plans for the weekend? I heard the
        weather isn't supposed to be (not / be) very good.

    B   Yeah. I'm supposed to go (go) to a family reunion, but I'm not really looking forward to it.

    A   Why not? Reunions are supposed to be (be) fun.

    B   Well, I'm supposed to make (make) 80 cupcakes. I was going to buy (buy) them, but my
        husband said that's cheating!

3. A   What did you do last night? Did you go out?

    B   No. I was supposed to cook (cook) dinner for a friend. I mean, I was not going to make (not / make)
        anything special, but then he called, and it turned out he was going to go (go) to soccer
        practice or something, so he didn't come. So I had a TV dinner! How about you?

    A   Actually, I was going to go (go) to a movie, but then I decided to stay home.

3 **Talk about it** Weekend fun

Group work Discuss the questions about this weekend.

▶ What's the weather supposed to be like?

▶ Are there any events that are supposed to be fun?

▶ Are you supposed to go anywhere or see anyone in particular?

▶ Are you supposed to do anything that you're not looking forward to?

▶ Is there anything you were going to do last weekend that you're going to do this weekend instead?

A What's the weather supposed to be like this weekend?

B I heard it's supposed to be nice.

1 Building vocabulary and grammar

A 🔊 2.03 Listen. Where are Luis and Rosa going? Do they want to go? Practice the conversation.

Luis Rosa, it's 6:00. We're supposed to be there by 7:00. Weren't you supposed to **get off** work early today?

Rosa Well, my boss called a meeting, and I couldn't **get out of** it. I had to go. Anyway, I don't **get it** – why is your cousin getting married on a Friday and not a Saturday, like everyone else?

Luis I don't know. All I know is that my mother will never **get over** it if we walk in late. So we have to **get going**.

Rosa OK. Uh, do you think I can **get away with** wearing pants?

Luis No way! It's supposed to be a formal wedding. Look, I got your silk dress ready for you.

Rosa Oh, I'll never **get used to** dressing up for these fancy weddings. Can we try to **get home** early?

Luis Rosa, I **get the feeling** that you don't really want to go.

Rosa Well, I just hope I can **get through** the reception.

Luis Oh, come on. Let's just go and enjoy it. It's a chance for you to **get to know** my family better. By the way, did you **get around to** buying a gift?

Rosa Weren't *you* supposed to do that?

Word sort **B** Find a *get* expression from the conversation above to complete each sentence below. Are the sentences true for you? Compare with a partner.

get around to	1. I was so busy last week that I didn't _get around to_ doing my homework.
Get the feeling	2. Sometimes I _get the feeling_ that people are annoyed with me for being late.
Get through with	3. It's hard for me to finish long novels. I just can't _get through with_ them.
GET IT	4. Why don't some people dress up for weddings? I don't _get it_ .
	5. I'll never _get used to_ wearing formal clothes. They don't feel right.
	6. I wish I could _get away with_ wearing jeans to work. They're so comfortable.

C Find six more *get* expressions in the conversation above. Write a sentence with each expression. Compare your sentences with a partner.

> 📙 Vocabulary notebook p. 42

get off - My sister gets off work early all the time.

Figure it out **D** Circle the correct choice to complete the questions. Use the conversation to help you.

1. Will Luis's mother **get over it** / **get it over** if they're late?

2. Rosa had to attend a meeting at work. Why couldn't she **get out of it** / **get it out of**? (AVOID)

3. Can Rosa get away with **wear** / **wearing** pants?

2 Grammar Inseparable phrasal verbs 🔊 2.04

Extra practice p. 143

With these verbs, the object always comes after the particle or preposition.

Verb + particle + object

Weren't you supposed to **get off** work early?
She'll never **get over** feeling embarrassed.
I'm sure she'll **get over** it.
I hope I can **get through** the reception.
I know you can **get through** it.

Verb + particle + preposition + object

Can **I get away with** wearing pants?
No. You can't **get away with** it.
Couldn't you **get out of** the meeting?
No, I couldn't **get out of** it.
Did you **get around to** buying a gift?
No, I never **got around to** it.

About you ▌ Complete the questions. Put the words in order, and use the correct form of the verbs.
Then ask and answer the questions with a partner.

1. If you weren't ready for a test, would you try to _get out of it_ (of / out / it / get)?

2. Do you find it hard to _____ (the day / through / get) without texting your friends?

3. Do you know anyone who tries to _____ (of / get / go / out) to parties because
    they are shy? Is it possible to _____ (get / feel / over) shy?

4. Have you ever told a "white lie" to _____ (of / get / an invitation / out)?
    Did you _____ (get / it / away / with)?

5. How do you feel about buying gifts? Does it take you a long time to
    _____ (to / get / choose / around) something?

6. Do you often argue with your friends? How long does it take you to
    _____ (over / get / an argument)?

7. Does it take you a long time to _____ (start / to / get / around) your
    homework assignments because you're on social networking sites?

3 Speaking and listening Going out

About you ▌ **A Pair work** Discuss the sentences below. Which choice is most like you?

1. **I'm one of those people who . . .**
   a. gets ready at the last minute.
   b. spends ages getting ready.

3. **When I go out, I always . . .**
   a. make an effort to dress up.
   b. try to get away with wearing jeans.

2. **If I'm late for something, I usually . . .**
   a. hurry to try to be on time.
   b. take my time and arrive late.

4. **If a friend cancels plans we made, . . .**
   a. I stay home and feel disappointed.
   b. I get over it and do something else instead.

B 🔊 2.05 Listen to Paula and Roberto talk about their plans for tonight. What happens?

C 🔊 2.05 Listen again. How would Roberto complete the sentences above? Circle his choices.

About you ▌ **D Pair work** What other habits do you have when you get ready or go out?

"I always say yes to invitations and then regret it and try to get out of them."

Sounds right p. 137

1 Conversation strategy Checking your understanding

A Check (✓) which statements are true for you. Tell the class.

☐ I love going to big parties where I don't know many people.

☐ I prefer going to small parties with a few friends I know well.

☐ I like going to parties with my co-workers or classmates.

B 🔊 2.06 Listen. How does Greg feel about parties?

Hugo So, there's another work party on Friday. You're going this time, right?

Greg I don't know. To be honest, I hate those things.

Hugo Really? Why's that?

Greg Well, I know it's supposed to be fun, but I'm just not very good at all that small talk.

Hugo So parties aren't your thing, huh?

Greg Not really. I just don't like big groups of people. I'd rather talk one on one, so . . .

Hugo So you're not going to go?

Greg No. I'll probably try and get out of it somehow. So, yeah. I'll just say I have other plans.

C **Notice** how Hugo checks his understanding. He asks questions in the form of statements. People often add *huh*, *right*, or *then* at the end of questions like these. Find more examples.

"So parties aren't your thing, huh?"

D 🔊 2.07 Read more of Hugo and Greg's conversation. Change the questions to "statement questions." Then listen and notice what they say.

Hugo So, aren't you going to show up at all? _So you aren't going to show up at all, huh?_

Greg No. Those work parties aren't my thing. Do you like them? _____

Hugo Yeah. But don't you want to network? You may get a promotion. _____

Greg Yeah. But I'm happy in my job right now. I'm not looking for a promotion or anything.

Hugo Oh. Don't you want to work your way up in the organization? _____

Greg Actually, um, no. Not really. So are you pretty ambitious? _____

Hugo I guess I am. But, the parties are fun anyway, and the people are interesting.

Greg So, do you know a lot of people in the company? _____

2 Strategy plus *SO*

You can use *SO* in many ways, including:

To start a topic, often with a question
So, there's another work party on Friday.

To check your understanding
So parties aren't your thing, huh?

To pause or let the other person draw a conclusion
I'd rather talk one on one, so . . .

To close a topic
So, yeah. I'll just say I have other plans.

> So parties aren't your thing, huh?

In conversation
So is one of the top 20 words.

A Find three places where you can use *so* in each conversation. Change the capital letters and add commas where necessary. Then practice with a partner.

1. A _____So,_____ ~~W~~what do you think of surprise parties?
                w

   B _____ I don't know. _____ I've never had one or been to one, _____so_____ . . . .

   A ___So___ No one has ever given you one? Do you think your friends would ever do that _____ ?

   B _____ No. My friends don't do that kind of thing.

2. A ___So___ Have you thrown any parties in the past year?

   B _____ Actually, yes. I had one last month. _____ A lot of people came.

   A ___So___ All your friends came?

   B _____ Yeah, they did. ___So___ It was great.

About you **B** **Pair work** Ask and answer the first question in each conversation above. Give your own answers.

3 Speaking naturally Being sure or checking

If you are sure:	*So your birthday's on Friday.* ↷	**If you are checking:**	*So your birthday's on Friday?* ↶
	So all your friends came. ↷		*So all your friends came?* ↶

A ◀)) 2.08 Listen and repeat the sentences. Notice how the intonation falls when you say something you are sure about and rises when you're checking information.

B ◀)) 2.09 Listen to four conversations. Are the speakers sure (S), or are they checking (C)? Add a period or a question mark, and write *S* or *C*.

1. So you go out a lot . (S)   3. So you don't like parties very much ? (C)

2. So you're a real people person ? (S)   4. So you never celebrate your birthday ? (C)
   so a able

About you **C** **Pair work** Ask and answer the questions. Check your understanding and use *so* where you can.

1. How often do you go to parties?   3. What do you do on Saturday nights?

2. Do you like to go out in large groups?   4. What do you usually do on your birthday?

1 Reading

A What kinds of behaviors are typical of extroverts and introverts? Make two lists. Scan the article for more ideas.

B Read the article. What does Susan Cain think our society can learn from introverts? Why?

> **Reading tip**
>
> Writers often use these words and expressions to say what people think or say: *argue, believe, contend, explain, according to* (*someone*).

EXAMINING the **"EXTROVERT IDEAL"**

"Solitude matters. And for some people, it is the air they breathe." Susan Cain, author of *Quiet: The Power of Introverts in a World That Can't Stop Talking*, firmly believes this to be true. She also believes that introverts struggle in our society because of the deep bias against them. She says that "our most important institutions, our schools and our workplaces, they are designed mostly for extroverts, and for extroverts' need for lots of stimulation."

According to Cain, introverts are sensitive to overstimulation and tend to enjoy quiet, contemplative environments. They think before they speak and are usually good listeners. In contrast, extroverts tend to be socially confident and quick on their feet.

Unfortunately for introverts, modern professional and academic settings are not planned with them in mind. People are expected to behave like extroverts – chatty, confident, and charismatic. Cain emphasizes that this proves difficult for those who identify as introverts – nearly half of all Americans – and they regularly face discrimination when they fail to act like their more outgoing counterparts.

In the competitive world we live in, Cain explains, there is pressure to stand out in a crowd. There is an expectation that being dominant will lead to success. As a result of this "Extrovert Ideal," workplaces and classrooms nowadays are often uncomfortable for introverts, who are frequently left feeling overlooked or disrespected. Collaborative brainstorming sessions are the norm. Talkers are considered smarter. Workers with strong "people skills" are praised, and "open plan" offices are common. While the assumptions that extroverts have better ideas or make better leaders are simply not true, introverts' valuable contributions are nevertheless likely to go unnoticed.

Furthermore, Cain contends that workplace innovation and productivity suffer when extroverts are valued more than introverts. In fact, research indicates that brainstorming in groups results in lower quality ideas, whereas there is a strong link between solitude and creativity. In general, open office plans reduce concentration, lower productivity, and make it difficult to retain good employees. "Our most important institutions are designed for extroverts. We have a waste of talent," says Cain.

Ultimately, Cain believes our society can learn a great deal from introverts. "It's a very powerful thing to be quiet and collect your thoughts."

C Can you find words or expressions in the article that mean these things? Underline them.

1. too much activity
2. thoughtful
3. on the other hand
4. charming and attractive
5. prejudice
6. look or be different
7. bossy or pushy
8. says or argues
9. keep (staff)

D Read the article again. Complete the sentences below with the correct information. Choose *a* or *b*.

1. Companies encourage their workers to be __*b*__ .
   a. introverts   b. extroverts

2. Cain believes extroverts are _____ .
   a. not valued enough   b. valued too highly

3. Self-assured people are more likely to be _____ .
   a. introverts   b. extroverts

4. The "Extrovert Ideal" means that introverts _____ .
   a. get fired   b. feel ignored

5. In open office plans, employees are more likely to _____ .
   a. leave the company   b. work harder

6. Cain believes that extrovert behavior leads to _____ performance in the workplace.
   a. better   b. worse

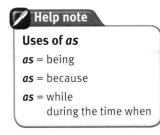

2 Listening and writing Extrovert or introvert?

A **Pair work** Take the magazine quiz. Then discuss your answers with a partner. Are you the same?

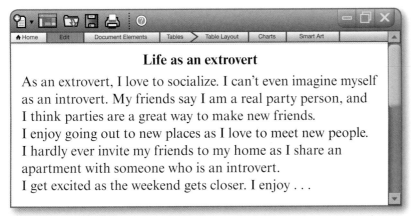

WHAT'S YOUR SOCIAL *STYLE*?		ANSWERS	
Do you prefer to . . .		Me	Jessica
① E a. go out and socialize?	I b. see friends at home?	① ⓐ b	a b
② X a. have lots of friends?	N b. have just a few close friends?	② ⓐ b	a b
③ T a. go out in a big group?	T b. go out with one or two friends?	③ ⓐ b	a b
④ R a. be the center of attention?	R b. keep a low profile?	④ a ⓑ	a b
⑤ O a. tell jokes and stories?	O b. listen as other people tell jokes?	⑤ a ⓑ	a b
⑥ V a. engage in chitchat?	V b. have more serious conversations?	⑥ a ⓑ	a b
⑦ E a. do tasks with others?	E b. figure things out alone?	⑦ ⓐ ⓑ	a b
⑧ R a. think of yourself as a "social animal"?	T b. think of yourself as an individual?	⑧ ⓐ b	a b

4a 4b

B 🔊 2.10 Listen to Jessica talk about her social life. How would she answer the quiz? Circle her answers.

C Read the extract below and the Help note. Circle the examples of *as*. What do they mean?

🔲 📇 📒 💾 🖨 ②	— ◻ ✕
♠ Home	Edit	Document Elements	Tables > Table Layout	Charts	Smart Art

Life as an extrovert

As an extrovert, I love to socialize. I can't even imagine myself as an introvert. My friends say I am a real party person, and I think parties are a great way to make new friends.
I enjoy going out to new places as I love to meet new people.
I hardly ever invite my friends to my home as I share an apartment with someone who is an introvert.
I get excited as the weekend gets closer. I enjoy . . .

> ✏ **Help note**
>
> **Uses of *as***
> *as* = being
> *as* = because
> *as* = while
>   during the time when

D Write a short article about your social style. Are you an introvert, an extrovert, or a little of both? Use *as* in your article.

E Read your classmates' articles. How many introverts are in your class? How many extroverts?

Free talk p. 131

Learning tip *Expressions in context*

When you learn a new expression, write an example sentence that uses it in context. Think of something you might want to say, and add ideas that set the scene or help you remember its meaning.

1 Complete the sentences using a *get* expression from the box.

[handwritten: algo que tenías que haber hecho y has hecho otra cosa que lo disimula]

get away with it	get it	get out of it	get to know →*[leame doed sh]*
get going →*start to live*	get off	get over it	get used to

[handwritten: to forget]

1. I'm late. I'd better __get going__ .

2. I love meeting new people. I think it's a lot of fun to __get to know__ people.

3. Weekends seem so short. I wish I could ___get off___ work early every Friday.

4. You're not supposed to go into clubs under the age of 18, but I know some kids manage to __get away with i.t__

5. I'll never __get away with__ *[handwritten: used to]* wearing a suit to work.

6. I don't understand why some people stay home all the time. I just don't __get it__ .

7. I was going to go to my class reunion. But I've decided to try and __get out of__ it

8. When I failed the exam, I thought I would never __get over it__ , but actually, I'm enjoying taking this class again.

2 Word builder Find out the meaning of the *get* expressions in the sentences below. Then write another sentence before each one that provides a context for the expression.

1. _____ She **gets on my nerves**. = *[handwritten: to bother you]*

2. _____ I just need to **get away from it all** so I can relax. *[handwritten: → no pensar en eso, nece... tar un espacio]*

3. _____ Maybe there's a way to **get around** that problem. *[handwritten: another option to solve a problem.]*

4. _____ I don't want to **get behind** on my payments.

[handwritten: no quedarte atrás]

On your own

Get a flip pad. Make different sections for common verbs like *get*, *go*, *do*, and *have*. Write as many expressions as you can for each verb.

go
- go nuts
- go bananas
- go crazy

Can Do! Now I can . . .

✓ I can . . .   ? I need to review how to . . .

☐ talk about going out and socializing.

☐ talk about things I am *supposed to* do.

☐ talk about things I think will happen or plans that changed.

☐ check my understanding with "statement questions."

☐ use *so* in different ways.

☐ understand people discussing their evening plans.

☐ understand someone talk about her social style.

☐ read an article about introverts and extroverts.

☐ write an article about my social style.

Law and order

✓ **Can Do!** In this unit, you learn how to . . .

Lesson A
- Talk about the legal age for activities using the passive of modal verbs

Lesson B
- Talk about crime and punishment using the *get* passive

Lesson C
- Organize your views with *First of all*, etc.
- Show someone has a valid argument with expressions like *That's a good point*.

Lesson D
- Read an article about privacy issues with smartphones
- Write a comment responding to a web article

Before you begin . . .

Do you have laws about these things in your country? What are they?

- Getting rid of trash and recycling
- At what age you can ride a motorcycle and what you have to wear
- Wearing seat belts and using a cell phone in a car

The Age of MAJORITY

In many countries, the law permits you to engage in new activities at the age of 18. We asked people what they think about 18 as the "age of majority."

When you turn 18, you can go see an "R-rated" movie – a movie that's restricted to adults. What do you think about that?

"What do I think? Well, I think the law ought to be changed – 18 is too young. Actually, I think R-rated movies should be banned altogether. They're far too violent."

– Bill Hughes

Do you think you should be able to get married before you're 18?

"No way. In fact, you shouldn't be allowed to get married until you're at least 21 or even older. Then there might be fewer divorces. Actually, I think a law should be passed that says if you want to get married, you have to take marriage classes first!"

– Maya Diaz

You can get your own credit card at the age of 18. Is this too young?

"I don't think so. I mean, young people have to be given their freedom at some point. You know, they ought to be encouraged to manage their own finances and things. They can always learn from their mistakes."

– Jared Blake

Do you think you should be allowed to vote at 18?

"I guess. I mean, you can do everything else at 18. Why not vote? It's too bad more young people don't vote, though. I think everyone should be made to vote."

– Aiko Nakano

The legal age for most things is 18, but in many places you can drive at 16. Is that a good idea, do you think?

"I must say I've always thought 16 is too young. Too many teenagers get involved in traffic accidents, and something really must be done about it. The legal age for driving could easily be changed to 18 or 21 or something like that."

– Pat Johnson

---

1 Getting started

To band = prohibide

A At what age can you do the following things in your country?

drive a car	get a part-time job	see a violent movie
get a credit card	get married	vote in an election

B 🔊 **2.11** Listen to the interviews above. What five things do the people talk about? Do they think 18 is the right age to start doing these things?

Figure it out **C** How do the people above say these things? Find the sentences in the article, and underline them. Do you agree with these views? Discuss with a partner.

1. They should ban R-rated movies.
2. They shouldn't allow you to get married until you're 21.
3. You have to give young people their freedom at some point.
4. They could easily change the legal age for driving to 18.
5. They ought to encourage young people to manage their own finances.

Grammar The passive of modal verbs ◀)) 2.12   Extra practice p. 144

> The passive of modal verbs for the present is modal verb + *be* + past participle.
>
> R-rated movies **should be banned**.   The legal age **could** easily **be changed**.
> You **shouldn't be allowed** to marry at 18.   Something **must be done** about it.
> They **have to be given** their freedom.   The law **ought to be changed**.

A Rewrite these comments about different laws. Start with the words given.

1. They should ban plastic shopping bags.
   Plastic shopping bags should be banned.

2. They ought to stop employers from reading employees' personal email. *Employers* should to be stopped.

3. They have to do something about all the litter on the buses and in subways. *Something* have to by Bas one done about ...

4. They shouldn't allow people to eat food on public transportation. *People* shouldn't be allowed to eat ...

5. They ought to fine people for making noise after midnight. *People* ought to be fined people –

6. They really must do something about speeding on freeways. *Something* must to be done

7. They shouldn't make movies with violent scenes. *Movies with* v.s shouldn't be made

8. They could encourage people to stop smoking if there were more anti-smoking laws. *People* could be encad

9. They have to do something about people who download music illegally. *Something* have to be done

10. They shouldn't allow children to quit school until they are 18. *Children* shouldn't be allowed.

> **In conversation**
>
> *Must* means "have to" in 10% of its uses. In this meaning, it is often used in expressions like *I must admit* and *I must say.*
>
> 90% of the uses of *must* are for speculation:
>
> *Things must be hard for couples who marry young.*

About you **B** **Pair work** Discuss the sentences above. Which do you agree with?

> A *Well, I agree that plastic bags should be banned – especially in supermarkets.*
>
> B *Yeah. They could easily be replaced with paper bags or something like that.*

3 Speaking naturally Saying conversational expressions

> *I mean, you can do everything else at 18. Why not vote?* **You know what I mean?**
> **You know,** *they ought to be encouraged to manage their own finances* **and things.**
> *The legal age for driving could easily be changed to 18 or 21* **or something like that.**

A ◀)) 2.13 Listen and repeat the sentences above. Notice how the expressions in bold are said more quickly, even when the speaker is speaking slowly.

About you **B** **Group work** Discuss the questions in the interviews on page 44. Use the conversational expressions above. Then decide on . . .

- three laws that should be passed.
- three things that people should be encouraged to do.
- three things people ought to be allowed to do.

> *"You know, something should be done about movie ratings. They ought to be made stricter. You know what I mean?"*

1 Building vocabulary and grammar

A 🔊 **2.14 Read the questions and answers on the website below. What questions are the people answering? Number the questions 1 to 8. Then listen and check.**

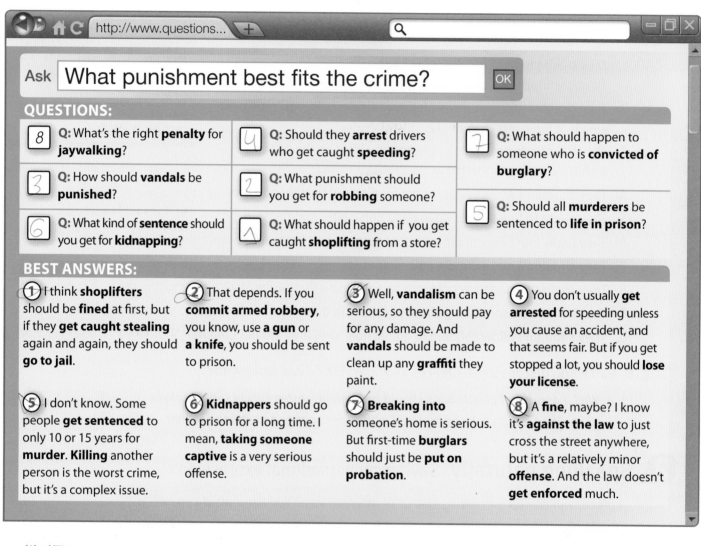

http://www.questions...

Ask **What punishment best fits the crime?** OK

QUESTIONS:

8 **Q:** What's the right **penalty** for **jaywalking**?

3 **Q:** How should **vandals** be **punished**?

6 **Q:** What kind of **sentence** should you get for **kidnapping**?

4 **Q:** Should they **arrest** drivers who get caught **speeding**?

2 **Q:** What punishment should you get for **robbing** someone?

1 **Q:** What should happen if you get caught **shoplifting** from a store?

7 **Q:** What should happen to someone who is **convicted of burglary**?

5 **Q:** Should all **murderers** be sentenced to **life in prison**?

BEST ANSWERS:

1 I think **shoplifters** should be **fined** at first, but if they **get caught stealing** again and again, they should **go to jail**.

2 That depends. If you **commit armed robbery**, you know, use **a gun** or **a knife**, you should be sent to prison.

3 Well, **vandalism** can be serious, so they should pay for any damage. And **vandals** should be made to clean up any **graffiti** they paint.

4 You don't usually **get arrested** for speeding unless you cause an accident, and that seems fair. But if you get stopped a lot, you should **lose your license**.

5 I don't know. Some people **get sentenced** to only 10 or 15 years for **murder**. **Killing** another person is the worst crime, but it's a complex issue.

6 **Kidnappers** should go to prison for a long time. I mean, **taking someone captive** is a very serious offense.

7 **Breaking into** someone's home is serious. But first-time **burglars** should just be **put on probation**.

8 A **fine**, maybe? I know it's **against the law** to just cross the street anywhere, but it's a relatively minor **offense**. And the law doesn't **get enforced** much.

Word sort **B** Make word webs like these. Add other words you know, and compare with a partner. Then discuss the crimes and say what punishments are appropriate.

Burglary
Robbery
murder Kidnapping
Speeding
Vandalism
Shoplifting
Vandal

(Crimes)   (Criminals)   (Punishments)   enforce a law (Other)

having a gun without a license   *shoplifter*   *get fined*

"Having a gun without a license is a crime."

📖 **Vocabulary notebook** p. 52

Figure it out **C** Circle the correct words to complete the sentences. Use the article to help you. Are the sentences true in your country? Discuss with a partner.

1. Murderers usually get **sentenced** / **sentencing** to life in prison.
2. Burglars who get **catch** / **caught** are never sent to prison.
3. If you are caught **shoplift** / **shoplifting**, you usually get **arrest** / **arrested**.

2 **Grammar** *get* passive vs. *be* passive ◀)) 2.15

Extra practice p. 144

The passive is usually formed with *be*, but sometimes you can use *get*.

People who speed **don't** usually **get arrested**.
Some murderers **get sentenced** to only 10 years.

After *should*, the *be* passive is more common.
People who speed should **be arrested** if they cause an accident.
Some murderers should **be sentenced** to life in prison.

Notice: Use *catch* (+ person) + verb + *-ing*.
What happens if they **catch** you **shoplifting**?
What happens if you get **caught shoplifting**?

In conversation

People use the *get* passive much more frequently in speaking than in writing.

A Complete the comments about law enforcement. Use the *get* passive or *be* passive with the verb given, and use the correct form of the verb after *catch*.

1. People who hack into computers should __be punished__ (punish) more severely. I mean, cyber crime is really serious.
2. Careless drivers hardly ever _get stopped_ (stop) by the police. The laws against speeding and other driving offenses should _be enforced_ (enforce) more strictly.
3. Lots of executives _get caught stolen_ (catch / steal) from their companies, and they often _get sent_ (send) to prison for a long time. White-collar crime is a big problem.
4. When vandals _get arrested_ (arrest), they shouldn't _be punished_ (punish) so severely. I mean, they should just _be sentenced_ (sentence) to a month of community service.
5. More people _get caught shoplifting_ (catch / shoplift) these days because of all the cameras they have in stores. But most shoppers are honest, and they really shouldn't _be recorded_ (record).
6. A big problem is that most criminals never _get caught_ (catch), and the ones that _get arrested_ (arrest) often _don't convicted_ (not convict).

Common errors

Remember to include *get* in *get* passives.

*Shoplifters often **get** fined.*
(NOT ~~Shoplifters often fined.~~)

About you **B** **Pair work** Discuss the opinions above. Do you agree?

3 **Listening** We got robbed!

A ◀)) 2.16 Listen to Jenny talk about a burglary. Answer the questions.

1. When did the burglary happen?
2. Who discovered it and how?
3. What was stolen?
4. Did the burglars get caught?

B ◀)) 2.16 Listen again. How does Jenny feel about the burglary? Check (✓) the sentences that are true.

☐ She never expected it to happen.
☐ She thinks it was inconvenient.
☐ She was scared.
☐ She thinks it was funny.
☐ She was upset.
☐ She felt disappointed with the burglars' punishment.

C **Pair work** Discuss the burglars' punishment in Jenny's case and the questions in Exercise 1A on page 46. What punishments are appropriate?

"Well, in Jenny's case, I don't think the punishment was severe enough. I mean, if burglars get caught, then they should be sentenced to at least two years in prison."

1 Conversation strategy Organizing your views

A Where do you often see security cameras? Make a list. Do you think they're a deterrent? If so, what against? Or are they intrusive and an invasion of privacy?

B 🔊 2.17 Listen. What do Adam and Selina think about security cameras on buses?

Adam	Did you hear they have cameras on all the buses now?
Selina	Yeah. They should be put in all public places.
Adam	So, you're in favor of them?
Selina	Oh yeah. For a couple of reasons. I mean, first of all, they're a good deterrent – people know they'll get caught if they cause trouble or whatever. And second, they make sure people pay.
Adam	Yeah . . . that's true.
Selina	And another thing is, for the drivers – especially late at night. I mean, basically, it's safer for them.
Adam	Well, you've got a point there. But on the other hand, don't you think all these cameras are a little intrusive? The thing is, it's like an invasion of privacy – someone watching you all the time.
Selina	I must admit, I never really thought of it that way.

C Notice how Selina and Adam organize what they say by using expressions like these. Find the ones they use.

Giving main ideas:	*(Well,) basically . . . The point / thing is . . .*
Adding ideas:	*Another thing is . . .*
Introducing a list:	*There are two problems . . .*
	. . . for a couple of reasons.
Ordinal numbers:	*First (of all), . . . Second (of all), / Secondly, . . .*
Numbers or letters:	*(Number) One, . . . Two, . . . or A, . . . B, . . .*

D Pair work Have a conversation about security cameras. Use these ideas or your own, and organize what you say. Take turns arguing for and against.

For security cameras
They help the police solve crimes.
They make people feel safer.
They're a deterrent.

Against security cameras
They're intrusive, and an invasion of privacy.
They're expensive. They're a waste of money.
They give people a false sense of security.

A Do you think there should be security cameras everywhere?

B Well, basically I think it's a good idea to have them. I mean, for a couple of reasons. First, . . .

2 Strategy plus *That's a good point.*

You can use *That's a good point* and other expressions like these to show someone has a valid argument – even if you don't completely agree:

That's true.
You've got a point (there).
I never (really) thought of it that way.

They're a good deterrent.

Yeah, that's true.

In conversation

That's true is the second most common expression with *That's*, after *That's right*.

A Respond to each comment. Use an expression above and add a different view.

1. I think metal detectors should be used in all public buildings. It'd be safer.
   You've got a point, but we shouldn't be made to go through one in every building.

2. If kids get caught skipping school without permission, then their parents should be fined.

3. More police should be put on the streets. That would help reduce crime.

4. Cameras should be installed in cars that teenagers drive. It could prevent accidents.

5. I think kids as young as 12 or 13 should be held responsible for their crimes.

B Pair work Take turns presenting the views above. Continue your arguments.

3 Listening and strategies Different points of view

A ◀)) 2.18 Listen to the class debate. Answer the questions.

1. Which of these topics is the class discussing? Check (✔) the topic.

☐ Raising the age limit to get married   ☐ Banning cars from city areas
☐ Sending dangerous drivers to prison   ☐ Raising the legal age for driving

2. What two arguments are given *in favor of* changing the law and *against* it? Take notes.

About you **B** ◀)) 2.19 Listen to five opinions from the debate again. Prepare a response to each point of view. Use an expression from the box, and add your own opinion.

1. _____

2. _____

3. _____

4. _____

5. _____

Useful expressions

That's a good point, but . . .
Absolutely! I agree with that.
Maybe, but on the other hand, . . .
That's a good idea.
I'm not sure about that for two reasons.

About you **C** Group work Discuss the topics in part A above. Organize your views, and remember to show that your classmates have valid arguments. Do you share the same views?

"I think the age limit to get married should be raised for two reasons. First of all, . . . "

(((• **Sounds right** p. 138

49

1 Reading

A What kind of privacy issues do people worry about? Make a list. Do you worry about them, too?

B Read the article. What types of information does it mention? Which of the ideas you discussed above does it include?

> **Reading tip**
>
> Articles sometimes describe the background to a problem and then list a set of problems and possible solutions.

http://www.smartphoneprivacy...

Is your smartphone too smart for your own good?

Gone are the days when a cell phone just made calls. We use our smartphones to text, take and post photos online, access email and social networks, get directions, check prices in stores, find nearby restaurants, and even find nearby friends. However, the risks smartphones pose can be underestimated. The truth is that smartphones are a bit too smart when it comes to gathering and sharing our personal information, such as location, contacts, messages, photos, and even financial data. Obviously, laws can be passed to protect us against invasions of privacy, but lawmakers simply haven't kept up with changes in technology. Why should anyone be concerned?

First of all, smartphone service providers typically save information about who you call, what messages you send, where you are, and much more. They often share this information with third parties, such as marketers who want to know your location, friends, and personal tastes. Ask your provider how to "opt out" of this part of your contract. Also, if you don't want your phone to keep track of your location, turn off this feature.

Second, your smartphone apps may be quietly collecting your private data. Perhaps this shouldn't be allowed, but it is. So before you download a new app, read the privacy statement. If it collects information that it doesn't really need, you probably shouldn't download it.

Third, think twice before you use the Wi-Fi in a coffeehouse as there's always a chance that someone will use illegal "malware" to spy on your private data, such as your bank account details. To avoid getting hacked, don't use public Wi-Fi to access sensitive personal information.

Finally, think about what would happen if your phone got stolen. Unless you have good password protection, your personal and financial data could be accessed immediately. Choose a password that can't easily be guessed. Also, don't let your smartphone remember your other passwords. Have every website request your password each time you access it. In addition, you can use programs that allow you to erase all the data from your phone if it's lost or stolen. Ask your service provider for information.

Laws may need to be passed to ensure smartphone privacy, but in the meantime, it's up to you to "outsmart" your smartphone.

C Find expressions in the article to complete these sentences.

1. You usually need to type in a password in order to ____access____ your email.
2. The risks of smartphones are often _underestimated_. People think they're safer than they actually are.
3. It's worrisome that apps collect private information without your permission. You should be _concern_____ .
4. The company that you pay for your phone service is called your _smphns service providers_
5. Sometimes you can _opt out_____ of certain parts of your phone contract — you can choose not to accept them.
6. Many apps know where you are as you move from place to place — they _____ of your location.
7. Criminals sometimes use _____ , or malicious software, to access your financial data.
8. If you use Wi-Fi in a coffeehouse, your computer could get _____ by a criminal.
9. You need to _____ your smartphone — and be smarter than your phone is.

D Read the article again and answer these questions.

1. Why are there so few laws against the invasion of privacy through smartphones?
2. What should you do in order to keep your location private?
3. Why do you think third parties want to know your location and personal tastes?
4. What should you do before you download a new app?
5. What two pieces of advice does the article give about passwords?
6. What else do you know about protecting your privacy?

2 Speaking and writing Posting a comment on a web article

About you **A** Pair work Answer the questions about the article on page 50. Take notes on your answers. Then discuss the questions with a partner.

1. What did you think of the article? Did you find the information relevant and helpful?
2. Are you concerned about all the personal information that is collected by smartphones?
3. Have you ever had a problem because personal information was shared by a service provider or app?
4. Do you know anyone who has gotten hacked by a criminal with malware?
5. What should be done about the invasion of privacy through smartphones?

B Read the comment below and the Help note. Underline the clauses that give reasons.

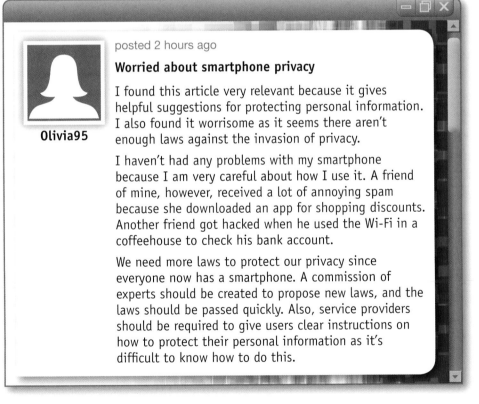

posted 2 hours ago

Worried about smartphone privacy

I found this article very relevant because it gives helpful suggestions for protecting personal information. I also found it worrisome as it seems there aren't enough laws against the invasion of privacy.

I haven't had any problems with my smartphone because I am very careful about how I use it. A friend of mine, however, received a lot of annoying spam because she downloaded an app for shopping discounts. Another friend got hacked when he used the Wi-Fi in a coffeehouse to check his bank account.

We need more laws to protect our privacy since everyone now has a smartphone. A commission of experts should be created to propose new laws, and the laws should be passed quickly. Also, service providers should be required to give users clear instructions on how to protect their personal information as it's difficult to know how to do this.

Olivia95

Help note

Giving reasons

You can use **because**, **since**, and **as** to give reasons.

> You can use **because** in all cases.

*I found this article very relevant **because** it gives . . .*

Use **since** only to give reasons the reader already knows or can guess.

*We need more laws to protect our privacy **since** everyone now has a smartphone.*

As is more formal.

*I also found it worrisome **as** it seems there aren't enough laws . . .*

C Use the notes you took in Exercise A to write a comment on the article on page 50. Give reasons for your comments.

D Group work Read your classmates' comments. Which do you agree with? Are there any ideas that you don't agree with? Discuss.

Free talk, p. 130

Learning tip *Word charts*

One way to write down new words is to use word charts. You can group related ideas together, which will help you learn and remember them.

1 Complete the word chart about crime using the words and expressions in the box.

burglar	murderer	steals from stores	paints on public buildings
murder	shoplifting	vandalism	breaks into a building to steal

Crime	Criminal	Activity
burglary		
	vandal	
		kills or murders people
	shoplifter	

2 **Word builder** Find out the meaning of the words below. Then make and complete a chart like the one above, adding more words and definitions.

| arson | blackmail | hijacking | joyriding | mugging |

 On your own

Look through an English-language newspaper, and highlight all the words that are connected with crime and law. How many of them do you already know?

 Can Do! **Now I can . . .**

| ✔ I can . . . | ? I need to review how to . . . |

☐ talk about what the legal age should be for different activities.

☐ discuss rules and regulations.

☐ talk about crimes and what punishments should apply.

☐ use expressions like *Basically, . . .* to organize what I say.

☐ use expressions like *That's a good point* to show someone has a valid argument.

☐ understand a conversation about a crime.

☐ understand a class debate about changing the law.

☐ read an article about privacy issues with smartphones.

☐ write a comment responding to a web article.

Strange events

✓ Can Do! In this unit, you learn how to . . .

Lesson A
- Talk about coincidences using the past perfect

Lesson B
- Talk about superstitions
- Show things in common in responses with *So* and *Neither*

Lesson C
- Repeat ideas to make your meaning clear
- Use *just* to make what you say stronger or softer

Lesson D
- Read an article about identical twins
- Write about a family story

1

When you see an unexplained object in the sky, you might be seeing _____.

2

When you have the strange feeling that you have been somewhere or experienced something before, you are having _____.

3

4

When you unexpectedly run into someone you know – for example, in another city – you call it _____.

When you can tell what someone else is thinking, you are experiencing _____.

Before you begin . . .

Complete the sentences with the words below.

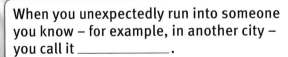

- telepathy
- déjà vu
- a coincidence
- a UFO (unidentified flying object)

Have you ever had experiences like these?

Do you know anyone else who has?

Have you ever experienced an
AMAZING COINCIDENCE?

"Oh, yeah, I think life is full of coincidences. I remember one time – I had just met my husband-to-be, and we hadn't known each other long. Well, he was showing me photos of an old friend that he hadn't seen or spoken to in years, a college friend who'd moved to Spain, Gerry. Anyway, there we were, looking at these photos, when the phone rang, and – you'll never believe it – it was his friend Gerry! He just called out of the blue."

—Emma Rivers

"Actually, yeah. One thing that sticks in my mind is . . . years ago, I was out in the Australian outback, driving through the desert. One night, I had set up camp and was cooking, and this van appeared out of nowhere with two guys in it. It was nice to have company because I hadn't spoken to anyone in days – I'd gone on this trip by myself, you see. Well, it turned out one of them had graduated from the same college I did. Small world, huh?"

—Glen Hutt

1 Getting started

A What kinds of coincidences happen to people? Make a list.

You meet a stranger, and you realize you both know the same person.

B 🔊 **2.20** Listen. What coincidences did Emma and Glen experience? Were they on your list?

Figure it out **C** Complete the answers. Use the anecdotes above to help you.

1. What did Emma find out about Gerry?   He _____ to Spain years ago.
2. Were Emma's husband and Gerry close?   Yes, but they _____ to each other in years.
3. Why was Glen alone?   Because he _____ on the trip by himself.
4. Why was Glen happy to have company?   Because he _____ to anyone in days.

2 Grammar The past perfect 🔊 2.21

Extra practice p. 145

> **Use the past perfect to talk about things that happened before an event in the past.**
>
> I **had set up** camp and was cooking, and this van appeared out of nowhere.
> I **had** just **met** my husband-to-be, and he was showing me photos . . . when the phone rang.
>
> **The past perfect is often used to give explanations or reasons why things happened.**
>
> It was nice to have company because I **hadn't spoken** to anyone in days.
> Gerry was a college friend that he **hadn't seen** in years. He**'d moved** to Spain.
>
> **Questions and short answers in the past perfect**
>
> **Had** you **gone** by yourself?　**Had** they **been** in touch?　Where **had** he **moved** to?
> 　Yes, I **had**.　　　　　　　No, they **hadn't**.　　　To Spain.

A Complete the stories with either the simple past or past perfect. Sometimes both are possible. Then practice with a partner.

1. A Have you ever been talking about someone and then they got in touch with you?

   B Yeah. In fact, last week I was talking about a friend who I _____ (not speak) to in a long time. I think he _____ (change) his cell phone and he _____ (not give) me the number. Anyway, he _____ (text) me out of the blue because he _____ (run into) my brother at a restaurant, and they were talking about me. So he _____ (decide) to get in touch. It _____ (be) great to hear from him.

2. A Have you ever been thinking about someone and then you've run into them?

   B Not really, but I experienced another coincidence recently. I _____ (go) to the post office because we _____ (get) someone else's mail. It _____ (happen) before, three or four times. So anyway, I was waiting in line, and I _____ (start) talking to this guy who _____ (come) in right after me. He was there because he _____ (not / receive) some of his mail. So I _____ (ask), "You don't know a Mr. Ling, do you?" And he said, "Yeah, that's me." I couldn't believe it! I _____ (have) his mail!

3. A Have you ever met anyone with the same birthday as you?

   B Actually, on my last birthday, my girlfriend _____ (decide) to take me to this restaurant that she _____ (go) to with some friends. I _____ (hear) about it, but _____ (not / have) a chance to go there. Anyway, we _____ (show) up at the restaurant, and my co-worker was there, celebrating her birthday, too.

About you **B** Pair work Ask and answer the questions above. Tell your own stories.

3 Listening It's a small world!

A 🔊 2.22 Listen to Elena tell a friend about a coincidence. Answer the questions.

1. Why had Elena joined an online chess forum?
2. What does she think about her online chess partner?
3. How had Elena and Derek met?
4. What did Elena discover about Derek? How did she find out?
5. What does Elena say about coincidences?

B Pair work Take turns retelling Elena's story. How many details can you remember?

1 Building vocabulary

A Read the superstitions. How many do you know? Do you have similar ones in your country?

SUPERSTITIONS FROM AROUND THE WORLD

TAIWAN If you see a crow in the morning, you will have a bad day.

JAPAN It's lucky to find a tea leaf floating upright in a cup of green tea.

THAILAND Dream of a snake holding you tightly, and you will soon meet your soul mate.

BRAZIL If you leave your purse on the floor, your money will disappear.

VENEZUELA If someone sweeps over an unmarried woman's feet with a broom, she'll never get married.

SOUTH KOREA If you give a boyfriend or girlfriend a pair of shoes, he or she will leave you.

ARGENTINA Pick up any coins you find, and you'll soon come into money.

PERU If you put clothes on inside out, you will get a nice surprise.

MEXICO If a bride wears pearls, she will cry all her married life.

TURKEY Your wish will come true if you stand between two people with the same name.

Word sort

B Complete the chart with the superstitions above. Add ideas. Then compare with a partner.

It's good luck to . . .	It's bad luck to . . .
find a green tea leaf floating upright.	*leave your purse on the floor.*

Vocabulary notebook p. 62

2 Speaking and listening Lucky or not?

A Do you know any superstitions about the things below? Tell the class.

 ☐ ___  ☐ ___  ☐ ___  ☐ ___

B 🔊 2.23 Listen to four people talk about superstitions. Number the pictures above 1 to 4. Is each superstition lucky (L) or unlucky (U)? Write *L* or *U*.

C 🔊 2.23 Listen again. Write down each superstition. Then compare with a partner.

3 Building language

A 🔊 **2.24** Listen. Is Angie superstitious? How about Terry? Practice the conversation.

Angie   Gosh, this looks good. I'm so hungry.

Terry   So am I. Could you pass the salt?

Angie   Sure. . . . Whoops! You know, it's supposed to be unlucky to spill salt.

Terry   It is? I didn't know that.

Angie   No, neither did I, until I read it on the Internet.

Terry   Actually, I don't believe in all that superstitious stuff.

Angie   Oh, I do. Now I always throw a pinch of salt over my shoulder if I spill it. And I never put shoes on the table.

Terry   Well, neither do I. But that's because they're dirty.

Angie   And I always walk around a ladder – never under it.

Terry   Oh, so do I. But that's so nothing falls on my head!

Figure it out   **B**   Find responses with *so* and *neither*. What do they mean? What do you notice about them?

4 Grammar   Responses with *So* and *Neither* 🔊 **2.25**

Extra practice p. 145

Present of *be*	**Simple present**	**Simple past**
I'm hungry.	I walk around ladders.	I knew that.
So am I. (I am too.)	**So do I.** (I do too.)	**So did I.** (I did too.)
I'm not superstitious.	I don't believe in superstitions.	I didn't know that.
Neither am I. (I'm not either.)	**Neither do I.** (I don't either.)	**Neither did I.** (I didn't either.)

In conversation

Responses in the present tense are the most common.

▬▬▬▬▬▬▬▬ *So / Neither do I.*
▬▬▬▬▬▬ *So / Neither am I.*
▬▬▬ *So / Neither did I.*
▪ *So / Neither have I.*
▌ *So / Neither was I.*

A   Respond to each of these statements with *So* or *Neither*. Then practice with a partner.

1. I'm not at all superstitious.   *Neither am I.*
2. I always pick up coins when I see them on the sidewalk.
3. I don't know many superstitions.
4. I didn't know the superstition about putting shoes on a table.
5. I'm usually a very lucky person.
6. I've never found a four-leaf clover.
7. I've always avoided walking under ladders.
8. I was superstitious when I was a kid.

About you   **B**   **Pair work** Take turns making the sentences true for you and giving true responses.

    A Actually, I'm a little superstitious.

    B So am I. But I think it's habit.   **OR**   *Really? I'm not superstitious at all.*

About you   **C**   **Group work** Do you believe in any superstitions? Tell the group. Are there any that you all have in common?

    "I always make a wish when there's a full moon."   "So do I, if I remember."

1 Conversation strategy Making your meaning clear

A Do you ever remember your dreams?
What do you dream about? Tell the class.

B 🔊 **2.26** Listen. What kinds of dreams does Olivia usually have? What about Hugo?

Hugo	Do you ever remember your dreams?
Olivia	Yeah, sometimes. I mean, occasionally, not every time, and I often have the same dream, too – you know, a recurring dream. Like I dream I'm sitting in a garden, waiting for someone.
Hugo	Yeah? Who?
Olivia	I don't know. I always wake up before they get there.
Hugo	Yeah? Is it upsetting?
Olivia	No, it's a nice dream, a happy dream. It's just a little strange. I always have pleasant dreams. They're never bad or scary or . . .
Hugo	So, you never have nightmares or anything?
Olivia	Not really.
Hugo	That's good. I often have weird dreams, really weird, I mean, just off the wall. Like I dream I'm falling or flying. Then I wake up and I'm like, "Whoa! Where am I?"

C **Notice** how Olivia and Hugo repeat their ideas to make their meaning clear. Sometimes they repeat the same words, and sometimes they use different words. Find examples in the conversation.

"I often have weird dreams, really weird, I mean, just off the wall."

About you **D** Complete each sentence by using a word from the list to repeat the main idea. Then discuss the statements with a partner. Do you agree with them?

fascinating	frightening	scared	terrible	unusual	worried

1. It's interesting to find out what dreams mean. It's _____ , actually.
2. Dreams about your childhood can mean you're anxious. You know, _____ .
3. You know, nightmares can be very scary. They can be really _____ .
4. Insomnia must be just awful. I mean, not being able to sleep is _____ .
5. It's silly to be afraid of the dark. I mean, there's no point being _____ .
6. Talking in your sleep is pretty common. It's nothing _____ . A lot of people do it.

2 Strategy plus *just*

You can use *just* to make what you say stronger. It can mean "very" or "really."

I often have weird dreams, just off the wall.

You can also use *just* to make what you say softer. It can mean "only."

In conversation

Just is one of the top 30 words. Over half of its uses are to make ideas stronger or softer.

It's just a little strange.

A 🔊 2.27 **Listen. Are these people using *just* to make what they say stronger or softer? Check (✓) the boxes.**

	Stronger	Softer
1. I often think about people and then they call me. It's just amazing.	☐	☐
2. I just love all those TV shows about telepathy. They're fascinating.	☐	☐
3. I don't believe people can read minds. They just make good guesses.	☐	☐
4. I believe you can make wishes come true. You just have to try, that's all.	☐	☐
5. I think people who believe in UFOs are just crazy.	☐	☐
6. I just don't believe in coincidences.	☐	☐
7. I don't really believe in luck. I just think people make their own good luck.	☐	☐
8. Coincidences are just events that you notice more than others.	☐	☐

About you **B** **Pair work** **Are any of the sentences above true for you? Tell a partner.**

"I often think about people and then I see them or they call. But I think it's just a coincidence."

3 Speaking naturally Stressing new information

*I have some strange **dreams** . . . some **weird** dreams. **Really** weird dreams. And they're **scary**. They're **always** scary.*

A 🔊 2.28 **Listen and repeat what the woman says about her dreams. Notice how the new information in each sentence gets the strongest stress.**

B 🔊 2.29 **Can you predict which words have the strongest stress in the conversation below? Underline one word in each sentence. Then listen and check.**

A Do you ever have bad <u>dreams</u>?
B You mean scary dreams? Like nightmares?
A Yeah. Dreams that make you all upset.
B No. I usually have nice dreams. Fun dreams. What about you?
A Oh, I never dream. At least, I never remember my dreams. So, do you ever have recurring dreams?
B Not really. My dreams are always different. But they're always happy dreams.

About you **C** **Practice the conversation above with a partner. Use your own information.**

🔊 **Sounds right** p. 138

Reading

A What do you know about twins? Make a class list.

"They can be identical." *"They're often very close."*

> **Reading tip**
>
> The title of a news article is often a summary of the story.

B Read the article. Why did it take so long for these identical twins to meet?

---

http://www.twinstories... +

SEPARATED at birth, then happily REUNITED

Elaine Logan and Mary Holmes the year they met for the first time

Like many identical twins, Mary Holmes and Elaine Logan are extremely close. They talk on the phone several times a week, and they spend holidays and vacations together. They're so close, in fact, that it's amazing to think that they didn't even meet until they were 30 years old.

Mary and Elaine were born in England after World War II. Their mother, who was renting a small room in a house, was unable to look after the girls. Another renter in the house, a soldier named Patrick Logan, adored the little girls, and with his wife, decided to adopt one of them – Elaine. The second twin, Mary, was adopted by another family from the Logans' hometown, the Blacks, on the condition that the two girls would never meet.

Nevertheless, the twins became aware of each other early on. When Mary Black was five, she saw a poster of some local school children. One of the children looked exactly like her. Mary thought it was a photo of herself. In fact, it was her twin sister, but her mother offered no explanation. Then, some years later during a doctor's visit, a little girl in the waiting room insisted on calling her "Elaine." Mary's parents decided it was time to tell Mary that she was adopted and that she had a twin sister in the same town. However, Mary's mother was still determined that Mary would never meet her twin.

Around the same time, Elaine Logan's mother pointed out a girl across the street one day. She explained that it was Elaine's sister, but that Elaine couldn't talk to her because the girl's mother wouldn't allow it. Elaine already knew she was adopted, but she was dumbfounded to find out she had a sister!

Mary decided not to contact her sister until she was 21 years old to avoid hurting her mother. However, at age 21, Mary got married and moved to Singapore. She still hadn't contacted her sister. Coincidentally, just three months later, Mary got word from a friend that her sister had tried to find her. Elaine had gone to the office where Mary had worked, but after learning that Mary was now in Singapore, she had left discouraged, and didn't even ask for Mary's address.

Several years later, after moving back to the UK, Mary figured out a way to contact Elaine. The two sisters spoke on the phone soon after and hit it off immediately. When they finally met, it was as if they had known each other all their lives.

By now, well over 30 years have passed, and it seems unimaginable that Mary and Elaine spent their first 30 years in totally separate worlds.

C Read the article again and answer these questions.

1. What condition did the Blacks set before they would adopt Mary?
2. How did Mary learn about Elaine? How did Elaine learn about Mary?
3. What happened the first time Elaine tried to contact Mary?
4. How did the twins feel when they first met in person?
5. In your opinion, why are identical twins often so close to each other?

D Find the expressions below in the article. Can you guess what they mean from the context? Match them with the meanings given.

1. look after _____
2. become aware of _____
3. insist on _____
4. dumbfounded _____
5. get word _____
6. hit it off _____

a. shocked and surprised
b. receive news
c. learn that something or someone exists
d. become friends quickly
e. take care of
f. continue to do something, though others disagree

2 Speaking and writing Amazing family stories

About you **A** **Pair work** Discuss the questions below. Do you have any family stories to tell? Write notes about a family story you have.

1. What's your family's background or history? Does your family have an interesting story?
2. How did your parents meet? How about your grandparents? What stories do they tell?
3. Does anyone in your family have an interesting profession? How did he or she get into it?
4. Are there any "colorful" characters in your family? Do you have any anecdotes about them?
5. Are you close to one particular member of your family? How did you become close?

B Read the article below and the Help note. Underline the four examples of prepositional time clauses.

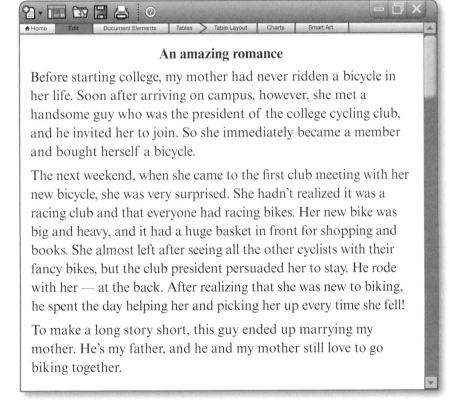

An amazing romance

Before starting college, my mother had never ridden a bicycle in her life. Soon after arriving on campus, however, she met a handsome guy who was the president of the college cycling club, and he invited her to join. So she immediately became a member and bought herself a bicycle.

The next weekend, when she came to the first club meeting with her new bicycle, she was very surprised. She hadn't realized it was a racing club and that everyone had racing bikes. Her new bike was big and heavy, and it had a huge basket in front for shopping and books. She almost left after seeing all the other cyclists with their fancy bikes, but the club president persuaded her to stay. He rode with her — at the back. After realizing that she was new to biking, he spent the day helping her and picking her up every time she fell!

To make a long story short, this guy ended up marrying my mother. He's my father, and he and my mother still love to go biking together.

Help note

Prepositional time clauses

Before starting college, she had never ridden a bicycle. = "Before she started college, she had never ridden a bicycle."

Soon after arriving on campus, she met a guy. = "Soon after she arrived on campus, she met a guy."

She almost left ***after seeing*** all the other cyclists. = "She almost left after she saw the other cyclists."

About you **C** Use your notes, and write a story about your family. Use at least three time clauses. Then read your classmates' stories. Which story interests you most? Tell the class.

Free talk p. 132

Learning tip *Grouping vocabulary*

A good way to learn sayings, like proverbs or superstitions, is to group them according to topics, using word webs.

1 For each topic below, find and write superstitions from this unit.

Dream of a snake, and you'll find your soul mate.

love

good luck

money

bad luck

2 **Word builder** Can you complete these superstitions? If you don't know them, you can look them up in quotation marks (" ") on the Internet. Then add them to the word webs above.

Bringing a new broom into a new house . . .
Cut your nails on Friday, . . .
Finding a ladybug . . .

If you open an umbrella indoors, . . .
Leave a house by the same door . . .
Putting clothes on with your left arm first . . .

On your own

Ask five people if they are superstitious about anything. Translate their superstitions into English.

ENGLISH
TEST
9 a.m.

✓ Can Do! Now I can . . .

✓ I can . . .   ❓ I need to review how to . . .

- ☐ talk about coincidences and superstitions.
- ☐ talk about the order of events in the past.
- ☐ give reasons for why things happened.
- ☐ show things I have in common.
- ☐ repeat ideas in other words to be clear.

- ☐ use *just* to make what I say softer or stronger.
- ☐ understand someone talking about a coincidence.
- ☐ understand conversations about superstitions.
- ☐ read an article about identical twins.
- ☐ write about a family story.

1 What are you supposed to do?

What do these signs mean? Write an affirmative and a negative sentence for each sign using *be supposed to*. Compare with a partner. Where might you see these signs?

A *This one means you're not supposed to use your cell phone. You're supposed to turn it off.*

B *Yeah. You're supposed to turn cell phones off in hospitals, I think. And on planes.*

2 You can say that again!

A Can you complete the second sentence so that it repeats the main idea of the first sentence? Add *just* to make the meaning stronger or softer. Compare with a partner.

1. I really enjoy going to parties. I ___just love going to parties___ .
2. I sometimes get a bit nervous when I meet new people. I _____ .
3. I don't go out every night because it's too expensive. It _____ .
4. I'm never on time when I have to meet friends. I _____ .

B Make the sentences true for you. Tell a partner your sentences. Use statement questions to check that you understand your partner's sentences.

A *I really don't enjoy going to parties. I just hate being with a lot of people.*

B *Really? So you prefer to stay home?*

3 Crime doesn't pay.

A How many ways can you complete the sentences below? Make true sentences.

Crime		Punishment	Criminals		Punishment
People who are convicted of	*shoplifting* usually get	*fined.*	I think	*shoplifters* should be	*fined.*

B **Pair work** Organize and explain your views. Say when your partner makes a good point.

A *People who are convicted of shoplifting usually get fined. I think shoplifters should be fined. First, because it's not a really serious crime, and second, . . .*

B *That's a good point. But I think sometimes shoplifters should be sent to jail for repeat offenses or when they steal something really expensive.*

63

4 A weird week

A Read the story and answer the questions below. Use the past perfect in your answers.

Last week, Eric had some bad luck and some good luck. Monday was a bad day. First, he saw a crow on his car when he left for work. After work, he went shopping with his girlfriend. She spent all her money on an expensive sweater, so he had to buy them both dinner. In the restaurant, Eric yelled at her for spending so much money, and she got very angry. On Tuesday, Eric bought her a gift to apologize – some sneakers – but she was still mad, and on Wednesday, she broke up with him.

On Thursday, Eric had a strange dream about a snake winding itself tightly around his leg. He didn't sleep well and overslept on Friday morning. He got dressed in a hurry and accidentally put his sweater on inside out. Later, while he was waiting in line at the bank, a woman behind him said, "Excuse me. Your sweater is inside out." He turned around and realized she was his old college friend, Sarah. He hadn't seen her since their graduation six years ago. What a nice surprise! Eric remembered his dream and suddenly thought, "This is the woman I'm going to marry."

1. Why did Eric pay for his girlfriend's dinner?
2. Why did Eric want to apologize?
3. Why did he oversleep on Friday morning?
4. Why was his sweater inside out?
5. Why was it a surprise to see Sarah?
6. Why did Eric have that last thought?

"Eric had to pay for his girlfriend's dinner because she had spent all her money on a sweater."

B Pair work Look at the superstitions on page 56. How might a superstitious person explain the events in the story? How many superstitions can you use? Discuss your ideas.

"Maybe Eric had a bad day on Monday because he'd seen a crow in the morning."

5 Get this!

Fill in the blanks with the correct forms of the *get* expressions in the box. Then practice the conversation.

get around to	get over	get through	✓get it	get the feeling	get used to

Ann My sister and her boyfriend just broke up. She's so upset.
Bill I don't _____*get it*_____ . They were the perfect couple.
Ann I _____ that she was expecting it. She'll _____ it soon.
Bill Did they ever get engaged? Or didn't they _____ it?
Ann They did, but she'll soon _____ being single again.
Bill It's a tough time, but she'll _____ it.

6 Things in common?

Complete the sentences and compare with a partner. Say if you are the same or different. If you are the same, use *So* or *Neither*.

I believe in . . .	I don't believe in . . .	I was going to . . .
Once I tried . . .	I'm not a fan of . . .	I'm not supposed to . . .

"I believe in UFOs."   *"So do I. I think I saw one once."*

UNIT **1** An interview with . . .

1 Think of interesting things to ask a classmate. Complete the questions below with your own ideas.

How long have you been _____ ?

When did you last _____ ?

What's your favorite _____ ?

Have you ever tried _____ ?

What do you like to _____ ?

Who do you _____ ?

What do you remember about _____ ?

What were you doing _____ ?

How did you end up _____ ?

2 **Pair work** Take turns asking and answering your questions. Give as many details as you can.

A *So, how long have you been living in this city?*

B *Oh, for about two years. My dad got a job here. He was working for this big company and . . .*

3 **Class activity** Share the most interesting questions and answers with the class.

UNIT **2** What's popular?

Group work Discuss the questions. Do you agree on your answers?

TV	Fashion	Cars	Hairstyles
• What TV shows are popular? • Have TV shows gotten better or worse in the last five years?	• What's in fashion right now? • Do you like the new styles as much as last year's?	• Which cars are popular right now? • What kind of car would you like?	• Which hairstyles are trendy right now? • How have hairstyles changed over the last few years? Has yours?

Music	Food	Technology	Personal tastes
• What bands are popular right now? • Have you downloaded any songs lately? Which ones?	• What diets and foods are popular? • Is your diet as healthy as it could be?	• What gadgets are popular at the moment? • What are some popular apps for phones and tablets?	• How have your personal tastes changed over the last five years – for example, in fashion, music, and food?

"Well, talent shows are still popular, but I don't watch them as often as I used to."

Free talk

Traditions

1 You have two minutes. Write ideas that your classmates might not think of.

Think of . . .

- a traditional instrument. _____
- a national holiday. _____
- a national sport. _____
- a traditional handicraft. _____
- a festival. _____
- a folk song. _____
- a national food or dish. _____

2 Pair work Ask your partner questions. Try to guess the things on his or her list.

A OK, so what is your instrument made from?

B It's made from wood.

A And where is it played?

Do you agree?

1 Pair work What is your opinion about the issues below? Think of two or more reasons to support your view on each topic.

"Well, to be honest, I think they should, for two reasons. First of all, . . . "

Do you think . . .	Name
1. manufacturers should be made to produce only energy-efficient appliances?	
2. consumers should be encouraged to stop using plastic bags?	
3. schools should be required to provide only healthy food for lunches?	
4. 16-year-olds should be allowed to vote in some types of elections?	
5. vending machines with candy and soda should be banned from schools?	
6. the speed limit should be reduced to 20 miles per hour (32 kilometers per hour) on all city streets?	
7. homework should not be given to students before high school?	
8. elementary school students should be required to take a national reading test?	
9. manufacturers should be forced to produce cars that don't use gasoline?	
10. the parents of children who regularly skip classes should be fined?	

2 Class activity Now survey your classmates. Find someone who answers no to each question. Find out why. Write his or her name in the chart above.

UNIT **4** **Pass on the message**

Class activity You are going to play a message game. Follow the instructions below.

STEP 1 Write your name on a piece of paper, fold it, and put it on your teacher's desk. Then pick another piece of paper from the pile. Read the name, but keep it a secret.

STEP 2 Think of a place you'd like to go with the person whose name you picked. Complete the chart with information about your plans.

a place you would like to go	
when you would like to go	
what you would like to do or see	
what the event is supposed to be like	
a time and a place to meet	
what the weather is supposed to be like	
what to wear	
how much it costs	
one thing to bring along	

STEP 3 **Pair work** Follow the instructions below, and then change roles.

Student A: Ask your partner to pass on a message to the person on your paper. Make sure you give all the details of your plans.

Student B: Listen carefully to your partner's message. You have to pass the message on later, so check your understanding!

A *Please tell Rodrigo I'd like to go to a concert in Riverside Park with him tonight. There's a band playing, and they're supposed to be really good. Tell him . . .*
B *Ok. Wait. So you're going to Riverside Park, right?*

STEP 4 Pass on the message you have just heard. Then listen to the message for you. Do you want to go to the event? Are you free?

"So, Rodrigo, Andrew would like you to go to a concert with him tonight. The band's supposed to be really good, and . . . "

131

6 What do you believe in?

Group work Discuss the topics below. What are your views?

Childhood beliefs Children often believe in things that are not true (e.g., the tooth fairy). What did you believe in as a child? What do you think about parents who encourage their children to believe in these things?

Good fortune Some people seem to be luckier than others. Why is this? Are you a lucky person? Tell about a time you were lucky.

Aliens A lot of people believe that there is life on other planets. Do you? Do you believe the stories about alien spacecraft that have been sighted around the world?

Coincidences Some people say that coincidences are just events that we notice. Other people think that everything happens for a reason. Do you agree? What coincidences have you or your friends experienced?

Dreams Some people think that dreams are a way of making decisions about your life – and that they tell you important messages. Do you agree? Have you ever "listened" to a dream?

"I used to believe in the tooth fairy. Every time I lost a tooth, I'd put it under my pillow. Then, in the morning, the tooth was gone, and there would be some money. Of course, it came from my parents! It's funny. But I think it's nice to keep traditions like that."

UNIT 1

🔊 **4.27** Listen and repeat the verbs. Is the stress in each verb like the stress in *bother*, *agree*, or *consider*? Write the words from the list in the correct columns below.

1. begin
2. continue
3. decide
4. expect

5. finish
6. happen
7. imagine
8. intend

9. offer
10. remember

• ● **bother**	• ● **agree**	• ● • **consider**
	begin	

UNIT 2

🔊 **4.28** Listen and repeat the pairs of words. Notice the underlined sounds. Are the sounds the same (S) or different (D)? Write *S* or *D*.

1. sh**oe** / c**oo**l __S__
2. b**oo**t / w**oo**l ____
3. fl**are**d / sc**ar**ves ____
4. atten**ti**on / styli**sh** ____
5. b**a**ggy / pl**ai**d ____

6. c**o**lor / s**o**lid ____
7. ca**sh**mere / fa**sh**ion ____
8. p**o**lka-dot / p**o**lyester ____
9. scr**u**ffy / c**o**mfortable ____

UNIT 3

🔊 **4.29** Listen and repeat the words. Notice the underlined sounds. Match the words with the same underlined sounds.

1. aff**e**ction __e__
2. b**ar**gain ____
3. d**ow**n ____
4. k**ee**p ____
5. p**oi**nt ____
6. sh**ow**ing ____
7. w**ea**r ____

a. b**are**foot
b. b**ow**ing
c. c**ar**ved
d. h**o**lding
e. **o**ffend
f. p**eo**ple
g. v**oi**ce

UNIT 4

🔊 **4.30** Listen and repeat the expressions. Check (✓) the expressions in which the *t* in *get* sounds like a quick *d*. (Hint: Look at the sound that follows *get*.)

✓ 1. ge**t** around to
☐ 2. ge**t** away with
☐ 3. ge**t** going
☐ 4. ge**t** home
☐ 5. ge**t** off

☐ 6. ge**t** out of
☐ 7. ge**t** over
☐ 8. ge**t** ready
☐ 9. ge**t** the feeling

Sounds right

  4.31 **Listen and repeat the words. Notice the underlined sounds. Which sound in each group is different? Circle the word with the sound that's different.**

1. against	arrest	freedom	(kidnapper)
2. invasion	probation	punish	should
3. killing	shoplift	vandalism	violent
4. caught	law	ought	young
5. jail	legal	majority	manage
6. license	prison	privacy	sentenced

UNIT **6** 4.32 **Listen and repeat the words. Notice the underlined sounds. These words have the sound /y/ or /w/ before the underlined sounds, although the letters y and w don't appear. Circle the correct sound.**

1. anyone	/y/ or (w)	7. language	/y/ or /w/
2. Australian	/y/ or /w/	8. music	/y/ or /w/
3. beautiful	/y/ or /w/	9. question	/y/ or /w/
4. coincidence	/y/ or /w/	10. quiet	/y/ or /w/
5. computer	/y/ or /w/	11. suede	/y/ or /w/
6. Europe	/y/ or /w/	12. unusual	/y/ or /w/

Extra practice

Lesson A Simple and continuous verbs (review)

A Complete the questions. Use the correct forms of the verbs given.

Common errors
Avoid continuous forms with verbs like *believe*, *know*, *like*, and *want*.

Have you known each other for long?
(NOT ~~Have you been knowing each other for long~~?)

1. What ___were___ you ___doing___ (do) at this time last week?
2. ___Did___ you ___play___ (play) a sport last weekend?
3. What kind of music ___do___ you ___like___ (like) nowadays?
4. How long ___have___ you ___been knowing___ (know) your best friend?
5. Who ___do___ you usually ___spend___ (spend) time with on weekends?
6. How often ___do___ you ___go___ (go) to the movies?
7. ___Have___ you ___travelled___ (travel) somewhere interesting on your last vacation?
8. How long ___have___ you ___been learning___ (learn) English?

About you B Pair work Ask and answer the questions above with a partner.

Lesson B Verb complements: Verb + -ing or to + verb

A Complete the conversations with the correct forms of the verbs. Sometimes there is more than one correct answer.

[margin notes: Mind Miss / Spend Finish / Imagine (or sth) / Be prep.]

Note
Notice the difference in meaning:

I remember paying the bill.
(I remember now – I paid it before.)

I remembered to pay the bill.
(I remembered, then I paid it after.)

1. A Why did you decide ___to study___ (study) English?
   B I'm considering ___getting___ (get) into hotel management, and hotels expect you ___to speak___ (speak) English well.

2. A What are you planning on ___doing___ (do) tonight?
   B Well, I'm thinking about ___going___ (go) to the movies.
   A Well, if you go, remember ___calling___ (call) me.

3. A Do you remember ___to meeting___ (meet) your best friend for the first time?
   B Let me think . . . I guess I don't remember the exact moment we met, but I know we really liked ___to play___ (play) together when we were little kids.

4. A What do you intend ___to do___ (do) next summer?
   B I'm going to stop ___working___ (work) at the beginning of August so I can spend a couple of weeks ___relaxing___ (relax) at the beach.

5. A Are you going to continue ___taking___ (take) English classes after you've finished this course?
   B Yes, I definitely want to keep on ___learning___ (learn) English!

6. A Do you remember ___to getting___ (get) your first-ever job?
   B Yeah. I worked in this new store. Luckily, I remembered ___to show up___ (show up) early, because they did the training an hour before we started.

About you B Pair work Take turns asking and answering the questions above.

Lesson A Comparisons with *(not) as . . . as . . .*

A Complete the *b* statements so they have the same meaning as the *a* statements.
Use *(not) as . . . as . . .*

1. a. Sneakers are more comfortable than boots.
   b. Boots _____ .

2. a. Women usually dress more fashionably than men.
   b. Men _____ .

3. a. I like pastels more than bright colors.
   b. I don't like bright colors _____ .

4. a. Long hair and short hair are equally stylish.
   b. Short hair _____ .

5. a. I spend very little money on clothes – the least possible.
   b. I spend _____ .

6. a. Women and men both have to work hard to look stylish.
   b. Men have to _____ .

7. a. When I buy shoes, I pay the most I can afford.
   b. When I buy shoes, I pay _____ .

8. a. Designer clothes and clothes from cheap stores can look equally stylish.
   b. Clothes from cheap stores _____ .

> **✕ Common errors**
>
> Don't use *so* instead of *as*.
>
> *She wears **as** many bright colors **as** she can.*
> (NOT *She wears ~~so many bright colors as~~ she can.*)

About you **B** **Pair work** Do you agree with the *b* statements above? Tell a partner.

Lesson B Negative questions

A Complete the negative questions in the conversations with
isn't, aren't, don't, or *doesn't.* Then practice with a partner.

1. A _____ you love these shoes?
   B I'm not crazy about them, actually. I mean, _____ that style kind of boring?

2. A ‹Aren't› _these glasses cool?   [handwritten: Are or is?]
   B Yeah, they're great. ‹Aren't› they kind of expensive, though?

3. A I'm thinking about changing my hair. ‹Don't› this a great style?
   B I don't know. _____ it seem too short?

4. A _____ this sweater seem a little too bright for me?
   I'm afraid I'd never wear it.
   B Really? _____ you like bright colors?

About you **B** **Practice the conversations. Replace B's lines with your own opinions.
Then change roles.**

Lesson A The simple present passive

A Complete the conversations. Use the simple present active or passive form of the verbs given.

1. A What __do__ people __wear__ (wear) during Carnival in Latin America?
   B Lots of people __wear__ costumes.

2. A What __do are__ Chinese children __given__ (give) by their parents on New Year's?
   B They __are are given__ red envelopes filled with money.

3. A What's the most popular sport that __is played__ (play) by men and women?
   B Well, soccer __is played__ by both men and women. So I guess it's soccer.

4. A What __do__ people __eat__ (eat) on Thanksgiving in the United States?
   B Most people __eat__ turkey.

5. A In Korea, __is__ Children's Day __celebrated__ (celebrate) in May or in June?
   B It __celebrated__ in May.

6. A What kinds of things __are bought__ (buy) during the holidays in the U.S.?
   B It depends on the holiday. Like on the Fourth of July, people __buy__ fireworks and stuff.

7. A What kinds of events __are held__ (hold) during the traditional festivals in Japan?
   B Well, people __dance__ (dance), and lanterns __are put__ (put) in front of the houses. It's really pretty.

About you **B** Pair work Write five questions about holidays or festivals in your country. Use the passive. Then take turns asking a partner your questions. Can you answer your partner's questions?

   A *So, when is the Dragon Boat Festival celebrated?*
   B *That's easy. It's celebrated in June.*

Lesson B Verb + -ing and to + verb; position of not

A Write the sentences about texting etiquette another way. Use verb + -ing or to + verb.

1. Texting during class is not acceptable. *It's not acceptable to text during class.*
2. It's impolite to text friends when you're having dinner with someone. _____
3. Texting too many times in a day can offend people. You can offend people by not texting too much
4. Not responding to a text message immediately is acceptable. _____
5. It's appropriate to read text messages during a business meeting. _____
6. Letting your text messages beep during a meeting is not acceptable. _____
7. It's OK not to spell words out in full in emails. _____
8. Sending a lot of texts to someone is bad manners. _____

About you **B** Pair work Discuss the statements above. Do you agree with them? Why or why not?

Lesson A *be supposed to; was / were going to*

A Rewrite the sentences with the correct form of *be supposed to* or *was / were going to*.

1. I expected my boyfriend to arrive at 7:00 tonight, but he didn't show up until 9:00.

   My boyfriend was supposed to arrive at 7:00, but he didn't show up until 9:00.

2. You should bring a small gift when you go to a friend's house for dinner.

3. I heard there'll be a storm this weekend.

4. I wanted to send out invitations to my birthday party, but I didn't have time.

5. My sister planned to have a party this weekend, but then she decided not to.

6. I'm planning to go to a concert tonight. My friends say it's going to be fun.

About you **B** Pair work Make a list of things you're supposed to do and not supposed to do in English class. Is there anything you were supposed to do last week for English class but didn't do?

Lesson B Inseparable phrasal verbs

A Rewrite the underlined parts of the sentences using an expression in the box.

get along with	get away with	get over	get through to
get around to	✓ get out of	get through	look forward to

get out of them

1. I find work parties boring. I usually try to <u>avoid them</u>.

2. It takes me ages to <u>find time to return friends' calls</u>. I'm surprised I have any friends. *get around to*

3. If a friend tells me a lie, I never <u>stop being upset by it</u>. I never trust that person again. *get over*

4. I'm not good at buying gifts for people, so I usually try to <u>avoid criticism and buy</u> gift cards. *get away with*

5. It annoys me when friends can't <u>make it to the end of dinner</u> without looking at their phones. *get through dinner*

6. My dad wants a big party for my twenty-first birthday. I hate parties, but he won't listen, and I can't <u>make him understand</u>. *get through to him*

7. My friends are all pretty easygoing. I <u>have a great relationship with</u> them all.

8. I like to spend Friday evenings all by myself. I <u>can't wait for</u> them.

About you **B** Pair work Make the sentences above true for you. Then read your sentences to a partner.

Extra practice

5 Lesson A The passive of modal verbs

A Complete the conversations with the active or passive form of the verbs given.

1. A I think 15-year-olds _____ (should / allow) to have jobs. They're old enough.

    B Well, I think they _____ (should / spend) their time studying, not working.

    A Yes, but I still think they _____ (ought to / give) a choice about whether to work. Some kids _____ (need to / earn) money, and they _____ (should / encourage) to work.

2. A People _____ (should / not / allow) to get credit cards until they're 21. They're not responsible enough.

    B But young people _____ (need to / learn) to manage their money, don't they?

    A Yes, but they _____ (not / have to / give) credit cards. They _____ (could / use) debit cards instead.

3. A Something _____ (ought / do) about dangerous drivers who've caused an accident. Maybe their licenses _____ (could / take) away for life or something.

    B But people learn from mistakes. They _____ (should / not / lose) their licenses forever.

    A Well, maybe they _____ (should / required) to take a driving test every year, then.

About you **B** **Pair work** For each conversation above, do you agree with speaker A or speaker B? Give reasons for your opinions.

UNIT

5 Lesson B *get* passive vs. *be* passive

A Complete the comments on transportation in other countries. Use the *get* or *be* passive with the verbs given. Both forms are possible.

> **Note**
> After a modal verb (e.g., *can*, *should*, etc.), you can use a *get* passive, but *be* passives are over 90 times more frequent.

1. People who _____ (catch) speeding in Norway can _____ (fine) 10 percent of their annual income. Sometimes they _____ (sentence) to 18 days in jail, too. That's pretty harsh. I mean, they should just _____ (sentence) to community service instead. – *Lars, Norway*

2. Here in Germany, people _____ (not / arrest) for speeding on the freeway because many areas don't have a speed limit. I love to drive fast, so I definitely think these laws should _____ (not / change). But you know, people _____ (fine) for running out of gas on the freeway. I guess it's dangerous, so . . . – *Lena, Germany*

3. It's interesting, but in some European countries, if your car breaks down, and you get out of the car without a visibility vest, you could _____ (fine). I really think laws like that should _____ (not / enforce). Actually, things like that should _____ (not / make) into laws at all. It should be your own choice. – *Jill, United States*

About you **B** **Pair work** What do you think about the laws above? What laws are there about driving in your country? Are they fair? Are there any laws that should be changed?

UNIT
6 **Lesson A** The past perfect

A **Complete the blog post with the simple past or past perfect. Sometimes both are possible.**

www.adrianbowensblog...

Was it a just a coincidence?   posted by Adrian Bowen

I have some good news for everyone! It's a long story, but . . . in my last year of high school, in California, I _____ (have) a girlfriend named Sophia. We _____ (meet) two years earlier when we were both playing on the softball team. After we graduated, she _____ (move) to Texas because she _____ (get) a place at a culinary school there. After a few months, she _____ (break up) with me because she _____ (meet) someone else. I was very upset, but I accepted it because we _____ (not / see) each other since graduation. Eventually I _____ (get) a job in Chicago. Before I left California, I _____ (try) to contact Sophia and her family, but no one _____ (return) my calls. Then, last month, I _____ (go) to the grocery store, and there was Sophia, in line at the checkout. It turned out she _____ (get) a job in Chicago a month earlier, and she _____ (move) into an apartment on my street! It was weird because I _____ (spend) a whole year trying to contact her. And the best thing was that Sophia _____ (miss) me, too. Anyway, to make a long story short, we're now planning to get married. Maybe it wasn't a coincidence after all!

B **Pair work** Read Adrian's blog again. Then close your books. Take turns telling the story. How much detail can you remember?

UNIT
6 **Lesson B** Responses with *So* and *Neither*

> **✗ Common errors**
>
> The past perfect is *had + past participle*. Don't use *had* + simple past.
>
> *I'd* just **seen** . . .
> (NOT *I'd just ~~saw~~* . . .)

A **Read the conversations. Circle the correct responses. There may be more than one. Then practice with a partner.**

1. A When I was a kid, I never went anywhere without my good luck charm.
    B Really? That's funny. **Neither was I.** / (**Neither did I.**) / **I did too.** / (**I didn't either.**)

2. A So many people claim they've seen UFOs, but I've never seen one.
    B **Neither have I.** / **I wasn't either.** / **I haven't either.** Actually, I don't believe they exist.

3. A I always make a wish before I blow out the candles on my birthday cake.
    B **I am too.** / **So do I.** / **I don't either.** But my wishes never come true!

4. A A few times, I've had the strange feeling I've been somewhere before – you know, like *déjà vu*.
    B **So have I.** / **I haven't either.** / **I am too.** It's weird, isn't it?

5. A I'm always losing things – my umbrella, my keys, and stuff like that.
    B **So am I.** / **So do I.** / **Neither did I.** / **I am too.** I guess we're both a bit forgetful.

6. A Something weird happened to me once. Like really weird. I had a dream, and it came true.
    B Really? **So did I.** / **Neither did I.** / **I did too.** / **I was too.** Actually, it scared me a little.

7. A Some people believe in telepathy, but not me. I don't believe you can read people's minds.
    B **Neither do I.** / **I'm not either.** / **I don't either.** I never know what other people are thinking.

About
you **B** **Pair work** Practice the conversations again, this time making the sentences true for you and giving true responses.

145

Illustration credits

Harry Briggs: 7, 31, 55, 68, 69, 95 **Bunky Hurter:** 14, 36, 54, 77, 100 **Scott Macneil:** 71 **Q2A studio artists:** 24, 47, 57, 79, 89 **Lucy Truman:** 10, 20, 30, 42, 52, 62, 74, 84, 94, 106, 116, 126

Photography credits

Back cover: ©vovan/Shutterstock **38, 39, 58, 59, 90, 91, 112, 113** ©Cambridge University Press **6, 7, 12, 26, 27, 70, 71, 80, 102, 103, 118, 122, 123** ©Frank Veronsky **viii** *(left to right)* ©RubberBall/SuperStock; ©Cultura Limited/SuperStock **1** *(clockwise from top left)* ©Marmaduke St. John/Alamy; ©Exactostock/SuperStock; ©Nicola Tree/Getty Images; ©Steven Robertson/istockphoto **2** ©Thinkstock; *(top background)* ©monticello/Shutterstock **3** ©Masterfile/RF **4** ©blackred/istockphoto; *(background)* ©ruskpp/Shutterstock **8** ©Jordan Strauss/Invision/AP; *(utensils)* ©Martin Kemp/Shutterstock **9** ©2010 AFP/Getty Images **11** *(clockwise from top left)* ©Blend Images/SuperStock; ©Radius/SuperStock; ©Transtock/SuperStock; ©Blend Images/SuperStock **12** *(all photos)* ©Frank Veronsky **13** ©Thomas Barwick/Getty Images **15** *(all photos)* ©Cambridge University Press **16** ©Imagemore/SuperStock **17** ©Imagemore/SuperStock **18** *(left to right)* ©quavondo/Getty Images; ©Dreampictures/Media Bakery **21** *(clockwise from top left)* ©Pixtal/SuperStock; ©miker/Shutterstock.com; ©Pixtal/SuperStock; ©Steve Vidler/SuperStock; ©Pacific Stock - Design Pics/SuperStock; ©windmoon/Shutterstock.com **22** *(clockwise from top left)* ©Gregory Johnston/age fotostock/SuperStock; ©Linzy Slusher/istockphoto; ©Thinkstock; ©Juanmonino/Getty Images; ©Thinkstock; ©Kerrie Kerr/istockphoto; ©Steve Kaufman/CORBIS; ©Marco Maccarini/istockphoto **25** ©Bill Sykes Images/Getty Images **28** *(background)* ©Shutterstock **29** *(all backgrounds)* ©Shutterstock **32** *(top to bottom)* ©Blend Images/SuperStock; ©4kodiak/istockphoto **33** *(clockwise from top left)* ©Chris Whitehead/Getty Images; ©Thinkstock; ©Thinkstock; ©PYMCA/SuperStock **34** *(clockwise from top left)* ©Thinkstock; ©Fancy Collection/SuperStock; ©Jupiterimages/Thinkstock; ©Edward Bock/istockphoto; ©Mie Ahmt/istockphoto; ©Exactostock/SuperStock; ©Silvia Jansen/istockphoto **35** ©Image Source/SuperStock **40** *(hole)* ©Fotana/Shutterstock **41** ©Nicole S. Young/istockphoto **43** *(clockwise from top right)* ©Transtock/SuperStock; ©Thinkstock; ©Exactostock/SuperStock **44** *(clockwise from top left)* ©Thinkstock; ©Thinkstock; ©Jupiterimages/Thinkstock; ©Jupiterimages/Thinkstock; ©Thinkstock **48** *(people)* ©Blaj Gabriel/Shutterstock *(bus stop)* ©Joy Rector/Shutterstock *(sign)* ©Rob Wilson/Shutterstock **49** *(top)* ©Blaj Gabriel/Shutterstock *(bottom)* ©Jack Hollingsworth/Getty Images **50** *(top)* ©Olivier Lantzendörffer/istockphoto; *(background)* ©Hluboki Dzianis/Shutterstock **51** *(background)* ©Hluboki Dzianis/Shutterstock **53** *(clockwise from top left)* ©The Power of Forever Photography/istockphoto; ©PhotoAlto/SuperStock; ©Thinkstock; ©Thinkstock; ©Ingram Publishing/SuperStock **54** *(left to right)* ©Paul Hakimata/Fotolia; ©Jupiterimages/Thinkstock **56** *(top section, top to bottom)* ©Eric Isselee/Shutterstock; ©Flavia Morlachetti/Shutterstock; ©Eric Isselee/Shutterstock; ©ULKASTUDIO/Shutterstock; ©Coprid/Shutterstock *(bottom row, left to right)* ©Morgan Lane Photography/Shutterstock; ©Peter Waters/Shutterstock; ©Eric Isselee/Shutterstock; ©Yu Lan/Shutterstock; *(background)* ©sunil menon/istockphoto **60** Photo Courtesy of Mary E. Holmes **63** *(left to right)* ©Arcady/Shutterstock; ©Arcady/Shutterstock; ©Miguel Angel Salinas Salinas/Shutterstock; ©Arcady/Shutterstock; ©Olga Anourina/istockphoto **64** ©altrendo images/Getty Images **65** *(clockwise from top left)* ©Yuri Arcurs Media/SuperStock; ©Exactostock/SuperStock; ©Niels Busch/Getty Images; ©Blend Images/SuperStock; ©baranq/Shutterstock; ©moodboard/SuperStock **66** *(clockwise from top left)* ©Michael Hitoshi/Getty Images; ©Jupiterimages/Thinkstock; ©Catherine Yeulet/istockphoto; ©Jupiterimages/Getty Images **67** *(invitation)* ©mark wragg/istockphoto *(photographer)* ©Marcin Stefaniak/istockphoto *(cake)* ©Dean Turner/istockphoto *(dress)* ©fStop/SuperStock *(flowers)* ©RubberBall/SuperStock *(passport)* ©Lana Sundman/age fotostock/SuperStock **73** ©Dfree/Shutterstock **75** *(clockwise from top left)* ©Thinkstock; ©Thinkstock; ©Thinkstock; ©Photo and Co/Getty Images **76** ©digitalskillet/istockphoto **81** ©BanksPhotos/istockphoto **82** ©Michael Rosenwirth/Alamy; *(background)* ©argus/Shutterstock **85** *(clockwise from top right)* ©Thinkstock; ©Jamie Grill/Getty Images; ©Fotosearch/SuperStock; ©Dmitry Kalinovsky/istockphoto **86** *(top, left to right)* ©WireImage/Getty Images; ©Julian Stallabrass/Flickr; *(bottom)* ©Photocrea/Shutterstock **88** *(background)* ©photolinc/Shutterstock **91** ©Bruce Glikas/Getty Images **92** ©stevecoleimages/istockphoto; *(background)* ©Loskutnikov/Shutterstock **97** *(clockwise from bottom left)* ©Getty Images; ©Indigo/Getty Images; ©Getty Images; ©GYI NSEA/istockphoto; ©GYI NSEA/istockphoto **98** *(top to bottom)* ©Featureflash/Shutterstock.com; ©Thinkstock; ©Ciaran Griffin/Thinkstock; ©Comstock Images/Thinkstock; *(background)* ©Henning Riemer/Shutterstock **99** ©Paul A. Hebert/Getty Images **101** *(top to bottom)* ©Getty Images; ©Time & Life Pictures/Getty Images **104** *(left to right)* ©GYI NSEA/istockphoto; ©Featureflash/Shutterstock.com; ©GYI NSEA/istockphoto **107** *(clockwise from top left)* ©Edward Bock/istockphoto; ©TIM MCCAIG/istockphoto; ©Johner/SuperStock; ©Thinkstock **108** *(top row, left to right)* ©Thinkstock; ©Comstock Images/Thinkstock; ©Thinkstock *(bottom row, all photos)* ©Thinkstock **110** ©Thinkstock **114** *(top to bottom)* ©Debby Wong/Shutterstock.com; ©Stockbyte/Thinkstock; *(background)* ©Itana/Shutterstock **115** ©Thinkstock; *(background)* ©Itana/Shutterstock **117** *(clockwise from top left)* ©Jack Hollingsworth/Thinkstock; ©Andrew Rich/istockphoto; ©Alexander Podshivalov/istockphoto; ©Blend Images/SuperStock **120** *(clockwise from top left)* ©Thinkstock; ©ViviSuArt/istockphoto; ©Neustockimages/istockphoto; ©Don Bayley/istockphoto; ©Thinkstock **124** ©age fotostock/SuperStock **128** *(left to right)* ©Rich Legg/istockphoto; ©daniel rodriguez/istockphoto; ©Stephanie Swartz/istockphoto **130** *(left to right)* ©Martijn Mulder/istockphoto; ©Corbis/SuperStock **131** ©Oliver Gutfleisch/ima/imagebroker.net/SuperStock **132** ©Ghislain & Marie David de Lossy/Getty Images **134** ©Monkey Business Images/Shutterstock **135** *(clockwise from top left)* ©hxdbzxy/Shutterstock; ©Sandra Baker/Alamy; ©bikeriderlondon/Shutterstock; ©ArtFamily/Shutterstock **136** *(background)* ©Gunnar Pippel/Shutterstock **141** *(top to bottom)* ©Thinkstock; ©Thinkstock; ©Lorraine Kourafas/Shutterstock; ©Chamille White/Shutterstock **145** ©Jupiterimages/Thinkstock

Text credits

The authors and publishers acknowledge the following sources of copyright material and are grateful for the permissions granted. While every effort has been made, it has not always been possible to identify the sources of all the material used, or to trace all copyright holders. If any omissions are brought to our notice, we will be happy to include the appropriate acknowledgments on reprinting.

8 Text adapted from "Blind Chef Christine Ha Crowned 'MasterChef' in Finale" by Ryan Owens and Meredith Frost, *ABC News*, September 11, 2012. Reproduced with permission of ABC News.
40 Quotes from *Quiet: The Power of Introverts in a World That Can't Stop Talking* by Susan Cain, Penguin Books, 2012. Copyright ©Susan Cain. Reproduced by permission of Penguin Books Ltd.